The Fire In My Soul

DELBERT McCOY

with

TIM SHEARD

This book is lovingly dedicated to Delbert's parents
Albert P. McCoy, Sr.,
And
Essie Mae McCoy

Seaburn Publishing Group
P.O. Box 2085
LI, City NY 11102

Cover designed by Andreas Kokkodis

ISBN: 1-59232-062-7

Library of Congress Cat. Num. in-Pub.-Data

Printed in the United States of America

www.seaburn.com

ACKNOWLEDGEMENTS

Delbert and Timothy wish to express our deepest gratitude for the help we have received from so many kind and loving people. Without their help, this book would never have been completed.

Monique and Kim, a special thanks. Without your love and support, Delbert would not have been able to keep on fighting and survive. To Gordie and Colleen Howe and Del Reddy, your encouragement and advice have helped more than words can say. Thank you. For Kate Lawson, a special thanks for writing about Delbert with grace and eloquence and for being such a good friend. To Katherine Combest, thank you for helping find and interview the detectives who made the arrests and the firemen who fought the blaze.

John Royal, Esq., thanks for your help in tracking down the transcripts to the trials of the arsonists. Robert Lippit and Roger Meyers, Esq., thanks for your legal support. To Renee Brandon, Delbert's companion, and Mary Lonergan, Timothys' wife, we offer our most humble thanks and enduring love. Charlene Brandon, we thank you for your support and help preparing the manuscript. To our many brothers and sisters, cousins and nieces and nephews, we send our gratitude for your support and your love.

Napoleon Ross, true friend and supporter, a special thanks. Walter Brandon, your constant support is gratefully appreciated. We gratefully acknowledge the help and support of Dr. Sandra Brown, who has given so much of her time and medical care to Delbert. For Drew and Mike, in the book of life, you are page one. We are grateful to Sam Chekwas of Seaburn Books for his faith in us and in Delbert's story.

Finally, we cannot adequately express our appreciation for the countless nurses, doctors, orderlies, therapists and other caring people who have helped Delbert through his many difficult times.

FOREWORD:

During our fifty years of marriage we have been very blessed to meet many unique people. Inside and outside the sport, our paths have led us to share moments with a number of special individuals who have overcome some extraordinary circumstances.

We have attended hundreds of charitable dinners, fundraisers and other noteworthy events where money is raised to help a particular organization, person, or noteworthy situation. During that time, we have been touched by the fortitude, desire, and incredible will that some people have to surmount their own particular setbacks.

Delbert McCoy is truly remarkable. He is Mr. Amazing in spite of some unbelievable obstacles. When he was originally injured, he survived when the odds of his survival according to doctors was only 1 in a 1,000! The technology for treating such horrendous burns and injuries at the time was not as advanced as it is today.

His 108 surgeries, the intense rehabilitation, the untold sleepless nights, anxiety, medication, physical therapy are mind-boggling.

In spite of these hardships, Delbert McCoy has not only survived and persevered, but he continues to be an inspiration to us and to thousands of other people. When you spend time with Delbert you can't help but smile at his infectious laugh, his gentle manners and his kind words that uses to make others feel better about themselves.

His story is a tale that demonstrates that incomprehensible obstacles can be overcome. His story is inspirational and powerful in that it will help readers know that there can be hope in the bleakest of situations. We predict greater and continued success for our friend, Delbert. He is truly a remarkable man with a remarkable story. In the book of life, Delbert McCoy is a Hall of Famer in a category all his own.

God Bless, and...HOWE! Mr. & Mrs. Hockey® Gordie & Colleen Howe

CHAPTER ONE

My name is Delbert Ray McCoy. I'm a fifty-one year old black man. I've lived my whole life in Detroit, Michigan—the Motor City. Back in 1968 I was a young fellow of nineteen holding down two full-time jobs. Me and my older brother Luther worked the midnight shift at the Warren Truck Plant on Mound, between Eight Mile and Nine Mile Road. That's a Chrysler facility. I worked in the brake department fixing assemblies.

You could make a good living in Detroit back then; there were plenty of jobs. When I got off work at six-thirty in the morning I'd walk across the street to the Chevy Gear and Axle plant on Nine Mile and work till three-thirty in the afternoon.

A year before, in the summer of 1967, we had the Detroit riots. A lot of people went crazy. My friend Napoleon Ross and I saw a guy coming out of a store with boxes of food and cigarettes. I asked him, "Did you pay for those cigarettes and stuff?"

He told me, "No, man, it's a riot!"

They set fire to stores and apartments and gas stations. There were flames shooting up into the sky all over the city. There weren't any fires set on my block, but from my bedroom window I could see the lights from the fires flickering in the night.

The mayor set a 6 PM curfew. My dad had us all locked down in the house. You didn't give him any argument, he was an ex-navy man, and he didn't play around. If he set a rule, that was it. We knew it was for our own good. We didn't even think about sneaking out during the riots.

In the morning I went over to check on my girlfriend, Yvonne. We stood on her aunt's porch on Dexter and watched army trucks and tanks rumble past her house. The soldiers walked behind the tanks, just like in Viet Nam. There were clouds of smoke rising from different parts of the city. It was scary.

But in nineteen sixty-eight, even though the city was scarred with abandoned buildings and empty lots, the auto plants were still going strong, and there was still a lot of work. People got married and raised kids, the kids went to school, and everybody carried on as best they could.

Being I was young and strong and full of energy, holding down two jobs wasn't that hard for me. My friend Lamont Lawrence—we called him Pug—he tried working at the Gear and Axle Plant, but he quit after a month.

"This work's too hard, it about wore me out," said Pug. "I don't know how a skinny guy like you can do two shifts day after day."

It's true, I was never a big strong fellow; I was always wiry. My mom worried that she couldn't put more meat on my bones. But as good as her cooking was, I never got really big. I'm not sure how I was able to work all those hours. Maybe it was because I played sports all my life. Baseball was my passion. I played it all year round, even in the snow.

I think the main reason I worked so many hours was because I had a wife and two children to support. Yvonne was home raising our daughters, and she was depending on me. Monique was one year old, and Kim—she's the baby—she was new born. Nothin' but a handful of love. I wanted to buy a house for them, so I was holding down the extra job and putting the second paycheck in the bank, saving for the down payment.

That was my idea of what life was is all about: raising a family and sending your children out into the world better off than you had it when you were young. I was young and happy, full of hope and promise. Just nineteen years old. I was optimistic about the future, with everything to live for, until the year turned the corner and January rolled in.

The New Year started out looking to be a good one for our family. There was fresh snow on the city, hiding the scars from the '67 riots. My baby girls were healthy and beautiful. And the money was coming in steady and strong.

Then in the middle of January my luck turned bad. The twelfth day of January, nineteen sixty-nine, is the day I was burned. I'm not talking about one of those freak accidents that scalds your foot or your arm, or even your face, and that hurts real bad, but then it's over. I'm speaking of a devastating injury. Of a burn that runs over you like a steam shovel, then backs up and crushes you all over again.

That day my life was shattered like a brick smashing into a beautiful mirror. I lost everything. My job. My independence. My dreams. It was all wiped away in a flash. Poof!

My wife and children changed, too. They looked at me different, and they thought about me like I was turned into somebody else. Somebody strange and disturbing. I was separated from my neighborhood. I lost the two jobs in the auto plants, along with all the satisfaction and security that a man gets when he's able to bring home a pay-check regular as clockwork.

My whole life was turned upside down and inside out. It became a nightmare I couldn't wake up from. It wouldn't do me any good pinching myself, either, I was already in so much pain that a little pinch wouldn't even have registered in my brain.

Yes, my life really changed on that cold January day. But it's funny, some things didn't change. The important things, the deep down soulful roots of my life didn't seem to change at all. Just the other day my good friend Napoleon Ross said to me, "You're the same Delbert I've known all my life. You still joke around and see the bright side of things . . .you must be crazy!"

Some people looking at me now might wonder what kind of man could survive such a devastating injury for all these years. They might find it difficult to see what part of me was left unspoiled and what part of me was ripped away by the fire. Well, if you let me tell my story, I'll try to explain it to you the best that I can. For although this is *my* story, unique in its twists and turns, it's also the story of an ordinary man who endured a terrible suffering simply because he was in the wrong place at the wrong time.

In other words, the catastrophe that fate visited upon me could just as easily have happened to you, or to somebody close to you. The story of my survival is the story of a common man who, supported by his family, his friends, and his faith, cheated death, and never gave up.

CHAPTER TWO

I grew up in a family that didn't have a lot of money. Some days there was no money at all. Even though we were poor in a material sense, we were rich in love and family togetherness. Everybody worked, even the kids. Because we all pitched in, we got by in hard times, and we enjoyed the good times all the more.

The first born was Albert McCoy, Junior. My folks called him June, and we call him that to this day. When June was growing up, he loved to dance. He was a great dancer. He always dressed real sharp. He drove sharp cars, too. From the time he started working full time he always drove a cool car. Usually a Cadillac.

The next born was Luther. When he was a baby my dad took to calling him Ball because he was just as round and plump as a ball. We called him that his whole life, until he died in 1974. He would be fifty-five if he were alive today.

Ball was tough. He didn't take any bull from anybody. He didn't get into fights or anything like that, he just spoke his mind and did what had to be done. Among the brothers, Ball was the bossiest. When they first met us, most people thought Ball was the oldest, because he would take charge of things. Nobody could talk Ball out of something once he made up his mind. Except for our father.

I was born on December 9, 1949. My mother was visiting her folks in Maysville, North Carolina. She named me 'Delbert' after an old family friend that lived down there. 'Ray' was her father's middle name. I stayed down south for about three weeks, then my mother brought me up to join the family in Detroit.

After me came Tony. We call him Slow. My dad gave him that nickname when Tony was ten or twelve, because he always took twice as long as the rest of us to do his chores.

Sometimes my dad would tell him, "You're just as slow as an old mule. You better move a lot faster or you'll get left behind." But he and my mom understood that Tony moved at his own pace, that was just his way, and most of the time they let him be.

Tony was the brother that everybody liked. He was just a loving guy who didn't have an enemy in the world. He was such an even-tempered kid that my uncle Pearlie called him Easy, because he would always take things easy and not let anybody get on his nerves.

After Tony came Jacqueline. She was always Jackie. Jackie

was outgoing. Fun-loving. She loved parties and getting dressed up. Jackie was something of a rebel. If my dad found out that one of us was past curfew coming home, chances are it was her.

As much as Jackie liked to have fun, she was also very generous. She would give a friend the shirt off her back. If somebody needed clothes, or food, or money—anything at all— she would see that they got it, even if it meant she had to do without.

The last born was Gwendolyn, who was always Gwen. She took after my mom. Gwen was patient, hard working, and very family oriented. She started working at Comerica Bank when she was 16, and she still works for them today.

Where Jackie was always outspoken, Gwen was the quiet type. Serious. She was also very thin, just like me. We took to calling her Skacie, because she was so skinny. She ate plenty, just as I always did, but she never put on much weight, even when she was pregnant.

That was our family. Six children in all, born to people raised on a farm who came north to Detroit for the work, for the adventure, and most of all, for a better life for their children.

In 1959, my dad bought a three-bedroom house at 3310 Northwestern. It wasn't a big fancy place; just a good, solid home where you could raise your children. He and his brother Pearlie McCoy poured cement in the front yard and put in a driveway for his car. Did it all by themselves. My dad called his brother Treetop because Pearlie was always as happy as a bird in a tree. Us kids wanted to make handprints in the wet cement, but my dad watched over the cement with that serious look on his face until the driveway was good and hard, so we never got the chance.

The elementary school and the high school we attended were both within a couple of blocks of the house. My parents picked the neighborhood so that none of us ever had to travel far to get to class. They wanted us to be safe and not have to walk a long way to get to school.

The two girls got one of the bedrooms, which was only fair. That left the four boys crammed into one room. We had two beds, with two boys to a bed. Albert (June) and Luther (Ball) slept in one bed, me and Tony (Slow) slept in the other.

Squeezing four boys into one little room can cause problems. Sometimes, when we went to bed, Ball would yell out, "June touched me!" because they bumped up against each other. Other times, Tony would say, "Delray's feet stink!" even when I'd washed up like I was supposed to, so it must have been *his* feet that were smelling up the bed.

A lot of the time I'd go to the dresser in the morning to get my shirt, and it would be gone! I'd look through the dirty clothes pile, but it wouldn't be there. Then I'd look up, and one of my brothers would have it on his back. I'd want to argue to get my own shirt back, but that's hard to do when I'd done the same thing the week before. How could I point a finger?

We loved to watch the cowboy shows on TV back then. We watched Gunsmoke, Rawhide, Bonanza, and Zorro. It was only natural for us to play cowboys and Indians a lot around the house. We used to have cowboy suits with the holsters and gun. We rode broomsticks for horses, running all through the house whooping and hollering. We would pretend to be Roy Rogers or the Lone Ranger. I liked to be the Cisco Kid, who was Spanish; I still don't exactly know why. We had pajamas with cowboys on them, and lots of toy guns, naturally. We weren't supposed to have cap pistols, but June had one, and when our dad found out, he got a whipping.

One time, Grandma Agnes McDonald was visiting. She was my grandmother on my mother's side. I was playing with my brothers when I said to Luther, "Wild Bill, get on your damn horse!"

My grandmother said, "Did he say what I thought he said?"

I got a whipping from my mom. It was a good thing my dad wasn't home, or I'd have got it ten times worse. My mom was gentle, and she didn't really whup us the way our dad did.

Us kids didn't get into too many fights with each other, my dad wouldn't allow it. He always told us, "We're family. We stick by each other, no matter what." We understood from the beginning that your family was precious, and we never forgot it. Not to this day.

One way we got along was, the four brothers tried to form a singing group, just like the Four Tops. We worked on *Under the Boardwalk,* by the Drifters, for weeks. We kind of tortured that song. All of our friends told us we stunk, even my best friend, Napoleon Ross. Eventually, we realized how bad we sounded, and we gave it up.

My sisters and brothers and I attended the Marr Elementary School. My brothers went ahead of me, so when it was my time to go, the teachers would say, "Another McCoy, eh? I taught your brothers, and I know your mother, so you better be good!"

The teachers didn't have to worry about me, I was a good student. My mom used to say that me and Luther were the smartest of the kids. When he heard that, Ball would say, "How come I have to work real hard and Delray hardly studies, and we get the same grades?"

My dad would tell him, "You got to work hard in life, there's no easy pickings. If it takes you longer to learn something, you'll remember it better, anyway."

In the elementary school I was a safety patrolman. I got to wear a bright orange belt across my shirt and hold a big red STOP sign. It was a good feeling helping the little kids cross the street, but the most fun was making the grownups in the cars wait while I held up my STOP sign. That got me to smiling inside, although I had to put on a serious face or the school would take away my STOP sign and my orange belt.

Being Captain of the Safety Patrol, I got to go to some of the Tiger games. I loved the Tigers, Detroit's major league team. They were my heroes. Sometimes the Safety Patrol got tickets for the bleachers, and we all sat up high and cheered our team. It was the best time a kid could ever have.

My parents, Albert, Sr., and Essie McCoy, were good, church-going people, and we all took after them. We attended the Oakland Baptist Church. My mom would get us all dressed up, ironing our clothes the night before. My sisters helped her get everything hung up and ready. Come Sunday morning, we all shined our shoes and combed our hair and really looked our best, and then my dad drove us to church.

We all went to Sunday school, and after that we joined in the service. All of us kids were in the choir at one time or another, and a couple of my brothers and I were in the boy scouts, too.

My dad believed that if we kept busy, we'd stay out of trouble and out of harm's way. He was very strict, but he was fair and he never played favorites. When he drew the line, you knew you better not cross it. My mom might bend the rules a little, she was the soft-hearted one, but with my dad, you did what you were told and no talking back.

We kept busy with jobs after school and during the summer, not just to stay out of trouble, but to help the family get by. My dad worked for Chrysler, and he was laid off quite often. Sometimes he'd have to wait for two or even three years before they called him back.

When he was laid off from the auto plant, he made do delivering papers, magazines, and telephone books. Any kind of work that put food on the table, he took it. He'd get us guys up early and we'd deliver the papers, him driving his old white '57 Dodge, then he'd drop us off at school. Everybody had to contribute to the family income. Nobody minded, it was just how you lived. We were family; we stuck together. The family was our strength.

One Christmas my mom took the girls and two of my brothers to her parent's place in Maysville, North Carolina. Tony and I stayed home with our dad. The only gift that we got was a checkerboard set. We appreciated it and didn't complain. Maybe we wanted something more, but we knew times were tough, my dad was out of work, and we played that checkerboard until the board was worn out, like steps in a museum.

We didn't have a lot of birthday parties, either. My birthday was so close to Christmas, my folks didn't see what sense there was giving me gifts right before the holidays, even when they could afford it. We understood right from the beginning there was no free lunch. My dad had to work hard to keep food on the table, and we learned to do the same.

At Northwestern High School I got good grades, but what I really worked hard at was sports. I mostly played baseball. I played first base or the outfield, and I was a good hitter. I could hit and throw from the right and the left, even though I was naturally a lefty. I could even spot the ball to any field: to left, center or right. My dream was to play professional ball with the Detroit Tigers. The coach, Fred Snowden, said I had a pretty good shot at it, and my mom and dad always told me there was nothing I couldn't accomplish if I worked hard at it.

While I was in my last year at high school I followed my next older brother Luther into the auto factory. Ball and I worked the midnight shift at the Chrysler Plant. The work we had at Chrysler helped out the family a whole lot. We were proud of that.

In the evening, I'd pack my school clothes and books, and Ball would drive us to work. In the morning I'd punch out, then I'd hop a ride to school with Ball, who went home to bed. I'd get through the day at school, then I'd play ball on the team. After that, I'd go home, get some sleep, and go off again to the plant to work.

After I graduated high school in June, 1967, I kept working at the Warren Plant from 10 PM to 6:30 in the morning. The auto companies had the best wages in Detroit. They were good union shops. Quite a few of my friends signed up, so you always had somebody to talk to. I'd usually get a ride to work and back home. Sometimes I'd go out for a beer with a couple of the guys after a shift.

Pretty soon, I took a second job right across the street at Chevrolet Gear and Axle working in the brakes and shoe repair shop. Lucky for me, by then I was chief steward at the Chrysler plant, so my first shift wasn't too physically demanding. I'd have to check on the guys and listen to any problems that came up. I'd write up a supervisor if he was breaking the contract, like ordering somebody to do something they weren't supposed to.

If a worker was having a problem with a supervisor, I'd go and look into it. First, I'd try and smooth things out, see if I could get the supervisor to lighten up the punishment. If that didn't work, I'd trade grievances. I'd take out some of the grievances we had against their side, and I'd offer to tear them up if they'd throw out the punishment for one of ours. A lot of the time we could work something out, everyone was happy, and the plant kept on going.

Those were long work hours, starting at ten at night and going until three-thirty the next afternoon, but I didn't mind. In fact, I was happy to have so much work. I could put a good piece of money away for that home I was going to buy for my family. Besides, you had to take the work when it was available, because you never knew when there would be layoffs.

I guess you could say I married kind of young. I was two months shy of my eighteenth birthday and Yvonne was sixteen when we got married. We had been going together for two years. We got along real good. We never had any fights worth speaking of. We loved each other, and we both wanted to have a big family, just like my mom and dad did, so I married her.

After living with my folks for a few months, we moved into an apartment, and before you knew it we had two little girls, Monique and Kim. The paychecks came in regular as clockwork. I put the money in the bank, Yvonne paid the bills, and I could provide for my growing family.

Life was so good. I couldn't wish for anything better. There was nothing I lacked; no place else on God's earth I wanted to live. The war in Viet Nam was going on, of course, and some of my friends had been drafted. I was classified 1-A, which meant that I was eligible, so I knew that if my number came up, I'd have to go. But I trusted in God and in good fortune, and I hoped it would be some other poor guy who would have to risk dying or being crippled in that faraway place of suffering.

I was happy, I had my mom and dad and brothers and sisters

close by, I had good friends to go hang out with, and my wife and daughters were my pride and joy.

Things couldn't have been better for me.

CHAPTER THREE

I was working at the Warren Truck Plant on the graveyard shift, 10 at night to 6:30 in the morning. One Friday my friend Napoleon Ross asked me if I wanted to celebrate his birthday with him on Saturday night. He suggested that we invite another friend, Lamont Lawrence, who we called Pug.

Nate was one of my best friends. His family moved into our neighborhood in 1960. He didn't play ball or enjoy watching sports on TV the way I did, he was into music. He played the violin. Even though he didn't follow sports very much, we became good friends right off the bat.

I was scheduled to be off from work on Saturday, and I didn't have to be back on the job until Sunday night, so I told Napoleon I could go with him as long as we didn't stay out too late. I needed to get some sleep Saturday night so that I could take my family to church on Sunday. We worshipped at the Oakland Baptist Church on Harper at Brush. I planned to go with the girls and my folks, then I'd get some rest before going in to work Sunday night.

On Saturday evening, Pug picked me up, and we went to a cabaret at the Ford Union Hall, Local 876, over on Twelfth and the Boulevard. A guy I went to high school with, Jimmy Edwards, and his group, the Superlatives, were performing at the Hall. Jimmy had told me about the show, and I really wanted to hear him. He was singing Motown. That was just about all we listened to back then. Pug and I were supposed to meet Napoleon later on at a teen dance club downtown called the Soul Expression.

After Jimmy's group got through, The Fantastic Four came out. They made it pretty big later on. Back then they just got their recording contract with Motown Records. You could tell they were going places, they had a great sound. Beautiful harmonies and original tunes that made you want to dance. The hall was really jumping when they performed.

Lamont and I hung out, talking to union friends when there was nobody on stage, and looking forward to meeting Napoleon later on downtown.

Eugene Kelley and Ronald Robinson, two young men from

15

Chicago, were visiting Robinson's sister in Detroit. They were dancing at a downtown club on Webster called the Soul Expression. The
Soul Expression was a teen hangout located on the second floor of an
old building above a dry cleaners. Admission was one dollar. You
entered the club from the street, then you climbed a flight of wooden
stairs. At the head of the stairs you bought a ticket, the ticket got you
admitted to the dance hall.

     The club didn't allow any alcohol or drugs; they only served
soda pop and snacks. To keep the kids from drinking, they had a strict
rule: if you left the club, you had to pay another dollar to get back in.
That discouraged the dancers from going out for a drink or a smoke of
marijuana in a parked car or in the alley behind the club. A bouncer
made sure you paid when you entered, and he'd remind you of the rule
if you wanted to go out.

     Kelley and Robinson left the club to meet their friends outside.
They sat with Theodore Wallace in his green Ford. Also in the car
were Ulysses Butts and Donald Jones, who were friends of Wallace.

     Earlier that evening, Robinson had borrowed Kelley's coat,
which he left it at the club. He went back to retrieve it. But the bouncer,
Alvin Gunn, would not let him back in. Robinson was drunk and ob-
noxious. Denied readmission to the club, he became belligerent, de-
claring that he didn't care about the club's rule, he wasn't going to
pay again to come back in.

     The fact was, Robinson didn't have another dollar in his pocket.
When the bouncer refused to let him back in the hall, he tried to push
his way back in. The bouncer made it clear: no money, no entry.
Robinson cursed him, promising revenge, then he stalked back down
the stairs and out onto the street.

     Outside the club on Webster, Robinson vowed to get even. He
told Kelley, "If they don't let me back in, I'm gonna burn the place
down." He asked his Detroit friend, Theodore Wallace, where was the
nearest gas station. Wallace had been driving Robinson and Kelley
around Detroit in his Ford. At Robinson's request, he drove the group
to the nearest gas station, then he waited while Robinson and Kelley
got out of the car.

     Robinson and Kelley told the attendant that they had run out
of gas and needed a can to carry it back to their car. The attendant
told them that was fine, he would sell them some gas, but they had to
leave a deposit for the can.

     With only enough money for a gallon of gas between them,

Delbert McCoy

Robinson needed something valuable that he could leave as collateral for the gas can. He removed a black onyx ring from his finger and offered it to the gas station attendant. The attendant agreed to hold it until they returned the container. He pumped two gallons of gas into the can, and then he watched as the two men got back into the green Ford and rode away.

At the Union Hall, Pug and I were talking to two girls I knew, Theresa and Ann. The Superlatives had finished their act, and we were waiting to see who was going to come up to the stage next. Theresa and Ann were going to drive home, which was just a few blocks from the Soul Expression, where Napoleon was going to meet us. I didn't want to miss Napoleon, so I told Pug I was catching a ride downtown with the girls. He agreed to meet me and Napoleon there later on.

Theresa and Ann dropped me off at the club on Webster. As I walked up to the entrance, I noticed a couple of guys talking in the street. I didn't make out what they were talking about, but they were angry about something, that much I picked up.

As I opened the door, one of the guys looked right at me and said something like, "I wouldn't go in there, man, we're fixin' on doing something." I didn't pay them any mind, I figured they would move on, so I went into the club.

Just inside the doorway was the stairs. There was a long line of kids waiting to go up, maybe twenty-five of us on the staircase. At the top of the stairs you paid your dollar and they let you into the hall. I stood at the end of the line waiting to buy my ticket, my dollar in my hand. There wasn't any drinking; just soft drinks and snacks. It was strictly music and dancing. A really nice place.

The stairway was packed with kids waiting to be admitted. Upstairs they were playing Marvin Gaye. He was singing *I Heard It Through the Grapevine.* Marvin's voice was mixed with the sounds of stomping feet and laughter. People were having a good time, and I couldn't wait to join them upstairs.

My friends Lamont and Napoleon would be joining me soon. We were going to dance and talk and celebrate Napoleon's birthday. I wasn't going to stay out too late. I had my family to take to church in the morning, and I'd be going back to work Sunday for the midnight shift.

I stood there at the bottom of the stairs with my back to the door, the last one in line, tapping my foot, ready to party. I was only there a couple of minutes, no more than that. Not paying much attention, I heard the door to the street open, then, I heard a loud *crack!* and the sound of breaking glass. Somebody had thrown a bottle through the doorway.

An instant later I heard a splash, and I felt something wet on my pants. That's when I smelled a terrible odor: *gasoline*. Before any of us in the hallway could react, one of the guys from the street threw a match onto the pool of gasoline. In a flash, the whole staircase and entranceway erupted in bright orange flames.

CHAPTER FOUR

When the flames erupted in the anteroom, the kids in the stairwell ahead of me started screaming and pushing up the staircase. They were falling over each other as they fought to get away from the fire. The door to the street slammed shut, *Bam*! The guys who had thrown the gasoline had run off into the night.

We couldn't go out through the door to the street, anyway, the vestibule was a sea of flames and thick smoke. We were all scrambling to get up the narrow wooden stairs, but they were slick with the gasoline, which was burning, too. Panic had us all desperate to escape the fire.

I looked down and saw flames licking at my legs. Being at the end of the line—the last one—I naturally got the worst of the gasoline splashed on me.

I tried to go up the stairs along with everybody else, but I slipped and fell. My shoes were wet with the gasoline, and that made them slick on the wet stairs. A few of the other kids had also stepped in the gasoline, and they were slipping on the steps, too.

I fell back down to the landing and into the pool of burning gasoline. My legs were already on fire from the gasoline, and when I fell, the fire spread to my hips.

It was a strange sensation, being on fire. I could see the flames rising up my body. I could feel the heat and the pain, but at the same time it almost didn't bother me, it was so unreal. It was like somebody else was going through it. Like it wasn't really me.

But it *was* me that was on fire. I was burning like a log tossed into a roaring fireplace.

Waiting in his green Ford outside the Soul Expression, Theodore Wallace sat with his two Detroit buddies. He was nervous, not liking what he knew Robinson and Kelley were doing. He had watched as the two men entered the club with the can of gasoline, but Wallace was too scared to tell them not to do it.

After a moment, Wallace saw Robinson and Kelley come running out of the door to the club. Seconds later, smoke and flames poured out from the doorway. Screams from inside the club pierced the cold January air, reaching the young men sitting in the car.

As the two arsonists jumped into the car, Robinson yelled at Kelley, "You threw the match too quick! The gas can exploded in my hands."

Robinson suffered burns on his hands. The hair on his head was singed as well, but Kelley was unscathed. As Robinson cursed his buddy and the club and the injustice he had suffered at the hands of the security guard over being barred from the club, Wallace put the car in gear and jammed his foot down on the gas pedal. The Ford sped away down Webster Avenue, disappearing into the bitter Detroit night and leaving behind the screams of the teenagers trapped in the hall.

The fire was filling the vestibule and marching up the steps. All the kids ahead of me on the stairs had made it to the top. Some of them turned around and called down to me. I could hear them yelling, "Get up! Get up! Run! Run for your life!" The flames were eating up the stairs and rising along the walls.

There was a Dry Cleaners on the first floor beneath the dance hall. The fire got into the chemicals they used. That made the fire even hotter and the smoke even more thick. The flames and the smoke got thicker and thicker.

That was when somebody upstairs in the dance hall threw a chair through a plate glass window at the front of the building. They had to do it, there was no other way out. The back door opened onto a roof, but the stairs going down from there were broken or missing. The window in the front was the only way out, so people started to jump down into the street two flights below.

The broken window let people escape, but at the same time, it turned the stairway where I was into a chimney. When the hot gases from the fire escaped out the broken window, it drew fresh air in behind it, and the fresh air fanned the flames. Pretty soon the flames in the stairwell turned into a fireball that raced up the stairs as hot as a blast furnace in a steel mill.

I ran up the steps as fast as I could. I was alone now, running through the fire like I was in the circus and jumping through burning hoops. The whole stairway and the walls were lit up, and the flames were swirling around, like they were alive. Like they wanted to dance with me in the fires of Hell.

Just as I reached the top of the stairs, the last wooden step collapsed. My left leg fell down into the stairway. I knew that if I went down those steps, I'd be a corpse. I pushed with all my strength. Somehow I got myself up onto the landing. I crawled onto the dance floor and collapsed, exhausted.

I was still on fire. The flames reached all the way to my neck and my face and my hair. Every part of me was on fire. I shut my eyes against the smoke and the heat, as I felt my strength melting away. A guy threw a coat over me as I lay on the floor and patted down the flames that were dancing on my skin. I lay there on the floor, unable to get up or even crawl away. All around me people were running and screaming and pushing to jump out the window.

It was a good drop out the window from the second floor onto the pavement. A lot of people were hurt landing on the sidewalk. Others pushed out the back onto a porch. A lot of the steps were missing from the balcony, so people jumped off into the alley, and they were injured by the fall, too.

Between the fire and smoke and the fall from the second floor, more than sixty people were hurt. I got the worst of it. As I lay on the floor of the dance hall, unable to move, with smoke all around me and flames coming through the stairwell into the hall, I could hear screaming and crying, and in the distance, a siren. I knew the fire department was on the way. All I could do was lie there. I was too weak to even crawl away from the smoke that was filling the hall.

The firemen came in through the broken window and found me on the floor. Right after that, two paramedics came up and gave me oxygen. They asked me my name and my telephone number. They wanted to let my family know what had happened.

I could tell them my name and my phone number, but after that I couldn't hear them very well. Their voices sort of faded out. I began to stare past the paramedics. I heard one of them say, "We're losing him!"

I fell into a deep pit, without any light or sound. It was the pit they bury you in. I lay in it for a long, long while.

CHAPTER FIVE

In the early hours of January 13, 1969, the Emergency Room at Detroit General Hospital was awash in a sea of injured people. By three a.m., the hospital staff was overwhelmed by the burn victims from the Soul Expression fire. Of the 250 teens at the Soul Expression that night, more than sixty of them were injured in the fire. Detroit General Hospital took over a dozen victims whose burns affected more than 50% of their bodies. Many were suffering from smoke inhalation as well. This all occurred on top of the normal crush of patients who crowded into a busy inner city Emergency Room on a Saturday night.

Dr. Thomas Grifka was the surgeon on duty that night at Detroit General. He called on doctors and nurses from several departments in the hospital to help. They spent hours assessing and treating the injured. They inserted intravenous catheters and gave the patients fluids, since burn patients become rapidly dehydrated.

Unable to admit all of the patients in their emergency room, they sent several of the victims to Henry Ford Hospital. All but one of the patients admitted were sent upstairs to the medical wards. The worst patient, Delbert McCoy, had burns over 85% per cent of his body. His body was charred as though he had been roasted over an open fire. The burns extended through the skin, fatty tissue and muscle. In some areas the burns extended down to the bone.

His burns were so extensive that he was scheduled for the Operating Room later that morning. In the OR they cut away, or debrided, the charred skin. Then they wrapped him in moist gauze and silver nitrate. The silver nitrate produces a bacteriostatic covering that prevents bacteria from colonizing the denuded tissues. Finishing with the debridement, the doctor sent Delbert to the Intensive Care Unit, where he was listed in extremely critical condition. He was not expected to live.

While I was in the Emergency Room at Detroit General, Alvin Gunn, the security guard from the Soul Expression, called my home. My sister, Gwen, answered the phone. The caller asked for my dad, and he came right to the phone.

"Mr. McCoy?" the guard asked.

"That's right," said my dad.

Delbert McCoy

"Mr. McCoy, there was an explosion at the club where I work, the Soul Expression, and your son Delbert was injured. He's in pretty bad shape. I don't think he'll make it till the morning, so you best go down to Detroit General right away."

A few moments later, a doctor from the hospital called the house. He told my dad I was burned real bad, and he should come down to the hospital. My older brother, Luther, was home. He drove my mom and dad to the hospital, but they couldn't get to see me for several hours. I'd been taken to the operating room, where they debrided me. The doctors took off all the dead skin, then they wrapped me in thick bandages and took me to the Intensive Care Unit.

Almost my whole body was burned. Seventy-five per cent of my burns were third degree, which meant the damage went all the way through the layers of the skin and into the muscle. The rest of my burns were second degree, which were serious, too. Every part of me was burned except for the soles of my feet and my genitals.

I woke up in a strange bed and looked around. I saw that I was in a hospital. I had bottles hanging on a pole with tubing going into me. One of the bags was bright red, and I knew right away I was getting a blood transfusion. That was really scary. To me, the blood meant that my injuries were serious.

I tried to lift my head, but I could hardly move it. My arms and legs felt dead, too. I could only move them an inch or so. Turning my head to the side, I saw somebody in a bed like mine. People in white coats walked by my bed not paying me any mind.

The doctor told me I was in the Intensive Care at Detroit General Hospital. It was the afternoon of the fire. I was on oxygen, I had intravenous lines running into my bloodstream, and I had a rubber catheter to drain my urine. Thick white bandages covered my whole body, even my arms and hands. Even my head.

I found out later that the doctor had called my family and told them to come down right away, that I was critical. My family had to wait over six hours to see me while I went through the debridement and then woke up from the anesthesia.

When I was over the anesthesia, the nurse told me that my family was outside waiting to see me. My mother, father, sisters and brothers were all gathered in the hall. My wife, Yvonne, her mom and her aunts were waiting to see me, too.

The surgeon in charge of my case, Dr. Thomas Grifka, told my family that he didn't expect me to live. He told them that he had never seen anyone burned as extensively and as deeply as me recover. My family understood that they should begin to make plans for my funeral.

So much of my skin was burned off that my blood and internal fluids were fast leaking out of me. The burns also left me completely unprotected from infection. The doctor explained to my family that without my skin protecting me, bacteria were already growing in the water and blood that was leaking out of me. In time, the bacteria would get into my blood stream and poison me.

I didn't know that the doctor was telling my family I was going to die. All I knew was that my injuries were very serious, what with all the bandages and the blood transfusion. Death was very close. My chances weren't good. I knew it. My family knew it. God knew it.

When the doctor was finished talking to my family, my dad was the first to come into the Intensive Care Unit. He'd been in the navy for the whole of World War Two, from 1941 to 1946. In 1945, my dad was stationed on an island in the Pacific waiting to invade Tokyo when he heard thunder way off in the distance. He found out later that the thunder was the atomic bomb dropping on Hiroshima.

He saw a lot of terrible things in the war, and he didn't let tough situations shake him up, so it was natural that he would be the first one in the family to come to my bedside. Many years after I was burned, my dad told me that he had seen a lot of men shot and blown up and burned in combat, but he'd never seen anyone in as bad a shape as me. I looked like a big, rotting egg plant. I was all swollen up and oozing fluids into my bandages.

My mother came in behind him. She tried to be brave, but I could see in her eyes that she was scared I was going to die any second, and my heart really hurt for her.

When they came up to my bed that first time, I mumbled, "Hi, daddy." They both stopped short and stared, they were so surprised that I could talk. My mouth was all swollen and I couldn't open it very far. That was all the words I could make. I don't think I said hardly another word during that first visit.

My mom couldn't stand to look at me for more than a minute. She told me, "The doctor says you're going to be fine, Delbert," but I knew from the look on her face and the trembling in her voice that it wasn't true. Not only that, but I saw that my dad was standing a little bit away from the bed, like he didn't want to come too close. I knew the doctor's words hadn't been good.

Pretty soon my mom went out in the hall and stood with my sisters, crying and praying for me, and expecting that I would soon be dead. My dad stepped closer to my bed. He kind of put his hand on my head, but he didn't say much, and I had the feeling that he was praying for my soul as if it was just about to go on its journey to Heaven.

My brothers and sisters came in next. They were allowed to visit two at a time. I was really shocked when my oldest brother June came through the door. June must have flown in that morning, because at that time he lived in New York City, where he had a business designing clothes. I was shocked he could get to Detroit so soon. I knew that, if he dropped everything and flew right out, I must be in really bad shape.

I asked June, "How do I look?"

He said, "You look all right. You'll be okay." But the look in his eyes told me I wasn't doing too good. My oldest brother couldn't hide his fear.

My wife and her mother came part way into the room, but they only looked at me from the doorway. They were both crying so much they could barely get out a couple of words before they turned and went out into the hall.

Then I saw my friend Lamont come into the room. I said to him, "Pug, you all right? I thought you was in the club."

"No, I never made it," he said. He explained that he went to meet a friend of his, thinking they would both go over to the club together. He heard about the fire on his car radio and went to the site to try and find out was I all right. Pug said the club was burned down by the time he got there, and he spent most of the night trying to find out what happened to me.

Napoleon came in behind Lamont. Nate was supposed to meet me at the Soul Expression, and I was worried about him, too. I thought he might have been upstairs when the fire started. Nate told me that after he worked the four to twelve shift he went home to change before going out to meet me, but he fell asleep. A couple of hours later sirens woke him up. Even though his apartment was more than two miles from the Soul Expression, the fire was so bad, they called in fire trucks and ambulances from all over the city.

It was the sounds of the ambulances and the fire trucks rushing to the fire that got him out of bed, although at the time he didn't know where they were going. By the time he learned what had happened, it was too late for him to go to the club and try and find me.

Both my friends tried to act like everything was okay, like I was going to be all right. But they had the fearful look in their eyes, just like June and my mom did. Their words were brave and encouraging, but their faces were already in mourning. The look in their eyes made me even more scared that I wasn't going to make it.

Once my family and friends were gone I was left alone with my thoughts. I knew that the Angel of Death was very near. His wings were spread out ready to carry me away. But I had a funny reaction to knowing that I was dying: I really didn't mind. I was very calm. If God was going to take me away, it was His will, and I could accept that.

The calm that came over me was partly due to all of the morphine they'd given me for the pain. Probably another part of it was because I was in shock, so my brain was not firing on all its cylinders, and I wasn't thinking as clearly as I normally would.

I lay there in the hospital bed thinking about my wife and my children. I thought about how much they needed me. I couldn't stand the idea that my daughters would grow up without their father. That they would never see me again. I didn't want to die and miss seeing the girls grow up into young ladies. And how would Yvonne cope without me bringing home the two paychecks? She was only seventeen. What would she do if I died?

I thought about how I'd been helping my parents ever since I got my first paper route. Even though I had a family of my own to care for, they knew they could always count on me when money got tight, which happened often enough. I didn't want to die before my parents did, that was wrong; it wasn't the natural order of things.

I could accept the dying. My soul would go to Heaven and I would be with Jesus. I just couldn't accept what it would do to my wife and my daughters and my parents. I had to live in spite of what the doctor was telling my family. I knew my chances weren't good. That things could go either way. But I wasn't going to give up, no matter how terrible my injuries were. My family needed me too much.

CHAPTER SIX

The Intensive Care Unit at Detroit General Hospital was a great big open room. There were curtains around the beds that the staff would draw closed when they worked on you. There was a bright spotlight attached to the wall, like in the operating room. When the doctors and nurses worked on you, they turned on the bright light. That light hurt my eyes, which were damaged from the fire, but I didn't complain because I knew they needed to see my wounds clearly. Besides, the light didn't hurt anything like the pain I felt when they worked on my burns.

My second day in the ICU, a pretty young nurse in a white uniform and a hat with wings came to my bedside. She was around twenty years old, not much more than that, and short, just five feet tall. She had dark hair and a big shining smile.

The young nurse introduced herself. "Hi! My name is Marlene. I'm going to take care of you today."

That smile and the way she talked to me: how can I describe it to you? It said so much to me, and it meant even more. You can't imagine how comforting her face was when she smiled at me and told me she was gong to be my nurse. It was like a rescue boat to somebody floating in the middle of the ocean with sharks circling around you. I felt better just knowing she was going to take care of me.

Marlene told me that when Dr. Grifka and his team came in she was going to help them change my bandages. That got me scared. I didn't know what was involved with unwrapping my dressings and putting new ones on, but it sounded like it would hurt a lot.

She told me she would give me morphine before the doctors started working on me, which would make me comfortable. They had me doped up pretty good already, and she would give me even more painkiller. I thought that would be okay.

Dr. Grifka was the surgeon who treated me in the Emergency Room. He was also the main doctor in charge of my case while I was in the Intensive Care Unit. He came to my bed with some other doctors, and they stood around my bed discussing my case.

He was a tall, broad-shouldered fellow, in his late thirties. He was serious, down to business. He didn't waste his time with a lot of small talk. He had a kind face, and his eyes were reassuring. I could see from the start that he cared about his patients, it was right there written on his face. He didn't have that stand-offish, formal doctor image that you expect. He never seemed to be in a hurry. He just looked like a nice guy who wanted to help you.

As the doctors stood at the foot of my bed discussing my case, I tried to follow what they were saying, but I couldn't understand most of it. When Dr. Grifka talked about "extensive third degree burns," I knew what *that* meant. And when he started describing the percentage of my body that was burned—"Seventy per cent one kind of burn, thirty percent another,"—I knew the fire had really torn up my body.

After he finished talking to the other doctors, Dr. Grifka came over and put his hand lightly on my forehead, sort of like when a priest blesses you. My head was covered in bandages. Only my eyes and mouth were exposed, but I could still feel his touch on my forehead.

The doctor spoke very softly and seriously, and he looked into my eyes when he spoke. The way he talked made me want to trust him right away, and I listened carefully to every word he spoke.

He told me I was going to make it. I was burned really bad, and it was going to be touch and go for a while, but I was going to pull through. I would have a lot of pain and need more surgery, but my chances were good.

His words gave me hope. Just as important, his touch lifted my spirit. That touch on my forehead. It was magic; like a faith healer. He touched me and looked into my eyes, and immediately I felt stronger and less frightened. Between his assurances and Marlene's optimism and warmth, I felt like I really was going to live.

I didn't know that the doctor was telling my family something completely different. He wanted to spare *their* feelings by not holding out false hope that I would live, and he wanted to spare *my* feelings by telling me I would make it. I needed hope, and my family needed to be prepared for the worst. For my funeral.

A little while later, Dr. Grifka and one of his assistants came up to the bed with a cart that was piled high with bandages. Marlene drew the curtains around my bed. She smiled, and then she gave me an injection of morphine. She put the needle right into the intravenous tubing, so the pain medication went directly into my blood. There wasn't any place to give me an injection in the muscle, everything was burned, although I didn't understand that at the time.

Marlene pulled the covers back, and for the first time I got a look at my body. Actually, all I could see was bandages. Even my head was covered with gauze. The only opening was a slit for my eyes and for my mouth. I was wrapped head to foot like a mummy in an old monster movie.

As soon as Marlene picked up my leg, pain shot through my body. I let out a groan. She looked worried. The doctor told me to hold tight, and he began to unwrap the dressings. They were soaked with blood. His assistant poured water onto my leg, which helped the dressing come loose; they were sticky where my blood had dried.

The pain was indescribable. I cried out for my father. "Daddy! Daddy!" I cried like a little child. I couldn't help it, the pain was unbearable. I couldn't look at what they were doing, either. I just shut my eyes and cried.

Dr. Grifka told Marlene to give me more blood. I needed another transfusion because I was bleeding so heavily, right through the bandages.

When they pulled the last layer of bandages off my leg, that's when the pain was the worst. Since I didn't have hardly any skin left, my nerves were exposed. Nerves are very sensitive things. Usually they're insulated by layers of fat and skin, but when they're exposed, like when a tooth has a cavity and the nerve ending is open to the air and the cold, that's when the pain shoots through you.

Each bandage they pulled off rubbed my exposed nerve endings. The longer they worked, the more the morphine wore off, and the pain kept getting worse and worse. I thought about those stories from the Bible, where the early Christians were nailed on crosses and stoned to death. They must have experienced the kind of pain that I did.

Halfway through the dressing change, Dr. Grifka told Marlene to give me more of the pain medicine. She went out through the curtains and brought more morphine, which she injected right into my bloodstream. I went into a sort of daze, half-awake, half-asleep. The pain kept waking me from my hazy state, but somehow I managed to let them change all of my bandages.

When they were done, Marlene drew back the curtains. She asked me if I was up for a visitor. I told her, "Okay," and that was when my friend Napoleon Ross came in to see me. It was a relief to see him, we were as close as brothers.

I asked Nate, "You think I'm gonna make it?"

"Course you'll make it, you're strong, Delbert Ray," he told me. "The Good Lord will get you through. I know it." He was so positive and sincere, I wanted to believe it. But the memory of the pain made me think things weren't going to good.

I felt a little better knowing that everyone was pulling for me. It lifted my spirits. It would be years before my friends and family told me that they were making arrangements for my funeral. That they had talked to people in the church about the wake and the prayer service for me. I only knew that the doctor said I was going to make it and that everybody was rooting for me.

Still, I was worried I would die that night. From the awful pain I had during the dressing changes it was clear that I was hurt really bad. I could see my blood running out of me as it soaked through the bandages. As soon as the doctor wrapped me in new bandages, they grew wet with blood, and the nurses had to hurry and hang more blood for another transfusion. I couldn't believe there was enough blood in the blood bank to keep me from dying.

Dr. Grifka didn't say much more to me the first few days in the hospital, other than not to give up. He told my family that my chances were one in a thousand, but to me he always said, "Hang in there, Delbert, just hang in there."

The doctors and nurses could see how bad my injuries were when they changed my dressings, but I didn't have the nerve to look. I closed my eyes and cried during the dressing change, and never opened them. I figured I was scarred pretty bad, but I really didn't have any idea how bad it was.

Whenever Marlene and Dr. Grifka changed my dressings, they had this very positive look on their faces. They never grimaced or showed any shock. They never shook their head. Never gave any sign that they were looking at some of the worst injuries they had ever seen, although that's probably what they were thinking. They always looked professional and calm, and they always reassured me that everything was going to be okay. That I was gong to get better, it was just a matter of time.

That first week in the hospital I heard a baby crying. There was a little baby girl in a bed across from me in the Intensive Care Unit. She was burned, just like me. Every once in a while I would catch a glimpse of her mother picking up the baby and walking with her up and down the room.

I asked Marlene if the baby was gong to be all right. She told me not to worry, the baby was going to be fine. For some reason, I started worrying about that child. I almost worried more about her than I did about myself. Each morning as soon as I woke up, I'd ask Marlene, "How's the little baby doing? Is she doing all right?"

Delbert McCoy

Marlene always told me the baby was fine, and I shouldn't worry about her.

There was also another patient who worried me. His name was Emmanuel. He was in a motorcycle accident. He was right across from me. I could hear him moaning all night. Toward the end of my first week in the hospital, the guy in the motorcycle accident died. When I saw what happened to him I figured that this was a place you went to die. I figured that I would probably end up the same way as the motorcycle victim. Dead.

I didn't want the baby girl across from me to die. I didn't want to die, either, but with most of my skin burned away and my blood running out all the time, it didn't look very hopeful that I going to beat the odds.

CHAPTER SEVEN

Dr. Grifka told my family that I had one chance in a thousand of surviving. My only hope was to get skin grafts. The grafts would be temporary; they would die and slough in a few weeks when my body rejected them. There was no way to prevent the rejection. But if I was lucky the grafted skin would slow the constant bleeding that was threatening to take my life, and that might give me time enough to let my body begin to heal and form new skin.

The skin grafts had to be donated from other people. Grafts from your immediate family were the best. They were the closest to my own skin, and my body would likely be slower to reject them. But even a graft from somebody who wasn't a relative would help to seal my leaking body.

The problem was, I needed a much bigger skin graft than one person could afford to give. In fact, I needed more extensive skin grafting right away than any of the doctors had ever done.

All my brothers and sisters volunteered to donate skin. So did most of my friends. The first to give were my youngest brother, Tony, and my friend, Alan Lawrence. Tony, who we call Slow, is a gentle soul who loves people. Giving comes natural to him. When we were kids Tony was always the last one to finish his chores, but this time, he wanted to be first.

My best, Napoleon Ross, wanted to donate skin, too. But when the doctors examined him, they found that he had bad veins, and so he wasn't a donor candidate. My older brothers, June and Ball, were scheduled to give the next round. After them, my sisters and my other friends would get their turn.

The second donor, Alan Lawrence, who we called Preacher, was the kind of guy who would do anything for a friend, no questions asked. Ball gave him the name Preacher because Alan looked a lot like a preacher we had in our church. It wasn't that Alan quoted the Bible all the time, although he went to church regularly, just as all of us did. We started calling him Preacher because of the resemblance, and the name stuck.

Doctor Grifka made the arrangements for Preacher and Slow to be admitted to the hospital and go to the operating room, where he would remove the skin and graft it on to me. Their skin grafts would help, but they wouldn't be near enough to stop the bleeding.

Once in a while the doctors were able to take skin from somebody who had just died. They call it "harvesting a cadaver." It sounded like the kind of thing we did at my grandparents' farm in North Carolina when we killed a pig and gutted it. Harvesting a cadaver wasn't as common in 1969 as it is today, because most people were uncomfortable donating the organs of their loved ones who had died.

In those days it was hard to find skin donors from cadavers. There's still a big shortage today, but back then people were even less likely to donate their organs when they died. They had to have signed a paper agreeing to the donation, and in 1969 it wasn't very common for people to do that.

As I lay dying in the hospital, a Mr. Eddie Kincannon called my dad at home. His family belonged to the Unity Baptist Church, which had fraternal ties with the Oakland Baptist Church, where we worshipped. Sometimes their minister would come and preach at our church; other times our minister would visit their church and preach to their congregation.

Mr. Kinkannon called my dad and said, "Mr. McCoy, I understand your son Delbert was in an explosion and he was hurt real bad."

"That's right," my dad said.

He told my dad that his own son, Paul Kincannon, had been involved in an armed robbery. A Detroit policeman shot his son in the head. It happened the same night that I was burned at the Soul Expression. The police said that when they spotted him the young man reached for his gun. "We'll never know for sure what really happened," Mr. Kincannon told my dad. "If he threatened the police or not. But the police shot him in the head, and now he's lying in a coma in the same hospital as your son."

Mr. Kinkannon told my dad that his son was never going to wake up from the coma. That he was brain dead.

"There's no hope for him," he said. "The doctors are fixing to pull the plug as soon as we give them permission."

The Kinkannon family was about to give the doctors the okay to take their son off life support when they heard about me. Mr. Kinkannon said to my dad, "Mr. McCoy, our son is gone. They're going to pull the plug on him any day, now. If there's any part of his body that we can give to your Delbert to help him survive, we'd like to do it."

My dad told Mr. Kinkannon that I needed an extensive skin graft. Without it, I would bleed to death. Mr. Kinkannon said that the doctors were welcome to use as much of his son's skin as was needed.

My dad thanked him very kindly. He told Mr. Kinkannon that his son, Paul, would be remembered in our family prayers, and that they would hold a prayer service in his memory at our church, the Oakland Baptist Church.

The father of the gunshot victim then called his son's doctors. He told them that he wanted his son's body to be made available for me. Those doctors talked to Dr. Grifka, and Dr. Grifka made arrangements to take me to the operating room. They had the Kinkannon boy in one room and me in another room. They had my brother Slow and Preacher in still another operating room.

Dr. Grifka and his team harvested patches of skin from my brother and my friend Preacher. They took it from the inside of their thigh and grafted it onto my body. Then they took a lot of skin from the Kinkannon boy. They wouldn't tell me how much skin they removed, but I heard later that the Kinkannon boy's skin covered half of my burns. One of the doctors who worked on me said that he had ever seen anything like it.

When the operation was over, they pulled the plug on Paul Kinkannon. I never saw him or met his family, but my dad told me about them when I woke up from the anesthesia. I was very grateful for the kindness that Mr. Kinkannon had shown me, even though I was sad that his son had died.

After Preacher and Tony gave the skin grafts, they spent the night in the hospital, then they were released. They stayed with my mom and dad for a few days, because they were sore and couldn't walk too good. My mom and my sister Gwen took care of them, while my dad was watching over me in the hospital.

Those first skin grafts slowed down the leak of blood and fluids from my wounds. I still needed several blood transfusions every day, and Dr. Grifka still was not very confident that I would survive. But at least now we had hope that the grafts would hold long enough for me to begin making new skin of my own.

Except there was one other problem. The doctor said I might need a hundred pints of blood before I was through with all the grafting and healing. I might need even more. That much blood was more than the hospital blood bank could get from the Red Cross for one patient. My case alone would strain the pool of blood they had for the whole hospital.

Once again, my dad came to my rescue, like he always did.

Delbert McCoy

His whole life he donated blood through the Blood Donor Program of the UAW—the United Auto Workers' Union. Because my dad had donated so regularly and for so many years, the Red Cross told him he was entitled to all the blood he or anybody in his family needed.

At the same time his friends in the UAW heard about my being burned. Right away, they started a blood drive in my name. If somebody had a different blood type than me, the Red Cross took the blood for somebody else and credited a pint to me. Between my dad's donations over the years and the other auto workers giving blood, there would always be plenty of blood available for me.

The deck was still stacked against me, I was still in critical condition, but the odds weren't quite so long. With the support of my family, the skin grafts from my younger brother Tony and my friend Preacher, the graft from the Kincannon boy who had been shot in the head, and with my faith in God, I knew I had a chance of surviving.

CHAPTER EIGHT

"Wait for your pitch, Ball!" I called out. "Wait for a good one!"

Ball—that's Luther, my next older brother—he was a pretty good hitter, so I wasn't worried about him striking out. I was on second base. I'd just hit a long shot way down the alley, which was pretty hard to do, considering it was twenty degrees outside and we were playing baseball on packed snow. We'd cleared out enough snow from the alley behind my house to let us run. We used the tops of garbage cans for bases. You couldn't get much traction to start for first, but, boy, could you ever slide.

That was one of the memories I played over and over in my mind those first days in the Intensive Care Unit. I had a lot of time on my hands to think, and so I thought about growing up, and when I thought about growing up, I always came back to baseball. Once I thought about baseball, I remembered how much I loved to play the game, whatever the season.

When I was young I could never get enough baseball. In the Spring I played on my high school baseball team. We were called the Northwestern Colts. When school was out, I played all summer. One time during a high school game the opposing team's batter hit a long high ball that looked like a homerun. I was playing outfield, and there was this fence along the back of the field. I jumped up onto the fence and caught the ball on top of it. Even though my legs were cut up pretty good, I still managed to hold onto the ball.

Everyone said it was a shame there wasn't any scout for the Tigers in the stands that day, they would have signed me up on the spot. My coach told me I really had a chance to try out for the Tigers. I was never happier than when I was playing ball and dreaming of being drafted by a major league team.

All through the Spring and Summer me and Napoleon would get up early and go to Cunningham's Drug Store to get the morning paper so that I could read the baseball scores. Cunningham's was right down the block on the corner from my house. I followed other sports, too, but baseball was what I loved the best.

One of my earliest memories was when the Yankees came to Detroit the year that Roger Maris was chasing Babe Ruth's record. It was 1961. I was twelve years old, and my dad explained how hard it was for anyone to beat the Babe's record. Even though we hated the Yankees—they were a rich team who beat the Tigers year after year—we still cheered for Maris, he had such a beautiful swing.

When I was a playing on the high school team, the Tigers had some of the best players in their history. They had Jake Wood and Denny McLain, Mickey Lolitch and Bill Freehan, Norm Cash, Dick McCauliffe and Willie Horton. It was a great bunch of guys, and Willie Horton was my favorite.

Willie was a young black man who graduated from my high school, Northwestern. Us kids were all rooting for him from the day he signed with the Tigers. We couldn't wait for him to be brought up from the Minors and play at Tiger Stadium. He had giant arms and powerful legs, and he hit for power. When he connected, the sound was like a cannon going off.

I remember the first time that the Tigers brought Willie up from the Minor League. It was in 1963. We couldn't wait for him to come to bat. But the manager had Willie on the bench inning after inning, and it looked like they weren't going to use him. That got us mad.

Finally, the manager brought Willie in as a pinch hitter in the bottom of the ninth against Robin Roberts. Willie crushed the ball. He hit it way up in the stands, and he tied the game. It was his first major league home run. I don't remember if the Tigers won that night, but Willie was everyone's hero. He was the rookie who sent one over the wall.

And now here I was in the middle of winter, with a nasty North wind blowing hard off the Great Lakes, bound and determined to play baseball as hard and as well as my hero, Willie Horton. The sky was gray, it looked like it was going to snow again any minute, but I didn't care, I was doing what I loved best: playing baseball. Even better, I was working on my fundamentals so I'd be ready to try out for the Tigers one day.

Me and my brothers had finished our chores earlier that morning. Everybody had to do chores on the weekend. We always argued over who got to use the mop, because that was the quickest chore to get done. Mopping was easy and fast. Other chores, like shoveling the steps and the sidewalk and the driveway, took an hour or even more, so nobody wanted to do that.

We were in a hurry to meet our friends and start to play, so there was competition to get the fast jobs. Tony, the youngest of us, always took his time. I didn't worry about him beating me, but Ball was the biggest and strongest, and he had a way with the broom or the mop that put me to shame.

I couldn't wait to get out and play ball. Baseball was my favorite sport. I couldn't get enough of it, playing ball, reading about it, or watching the game on TV. Any day that I could be around baseball, I was happy.

I was a switch hitter and a switch thrower. I could swing a bat from either side of the plate, and I could throw well with either hand. When I wasn't working for my dad or doing homework, I had a glove or a bat in my hand.

June—that's my older brother Albert, Jr.—he had just discovered girls, so he wasn't as regular a player as he used to be. But this time I got him to come out, and he was pitching to Ball, my next older brother.

My friend Napoleon Ross wasn't playing, it was way too cold for him. He didn't go out for sports. Nate was into music. He played the violin, and he was a great dancer. Even though he never liked playing sports, since he was my best friend he joined the game from time to time.

Nate had a very bad upper cut in his swing. He always started his swing too low and then pulled the bat up just as he got the head of the bat around and over the plate. As a result, he hit a lot of pop flies, when he connected with the ball, which wasn't all that often.

Anyway, Nate wasn't playing ball that day, it was the middle of a Michigan winter, and there were limits to even our friendship. But there were lots of other guys who loved to play, snow or no snow. I'd gone around the neighborhood recruiting kids, and now we had enough for a game.

I gave each kid a sports nickname. I don't know why, exactly. I guess it was because a lot of the great ball players had nicknames. Like Lou Gehrig, the Iron Horse. Or Babe Ruth, the Bambino.

My dad had always given people in the family nicknames, so I sort of took after him without even realizing it. Chuck was Chase, Shorty was Flyboy, because he hit a lot of fly balls. Dennis was Bop. Luther already had his nickname, (Ball), as did Albert (June), and Tony (Slow), so we let them keep their old nicknames, but everybody else got new ones.

I wasn't the only one giving out nicknames. Around that time the guys started to call me Delco, after the battery manufacturer that was based in Detroit, because I was always full of energy. I'd organize a game in the middle of winter, even getting everybody to help shovel out the alley. Most of all, I always played hard. Full-throttle.

"You're just like the Delco battery, you never run out of energy," they said, so that became my baseball nickname.

On this cold Michigan day, Ball got a pretty good hit. The ball went scooting along the ice, bouncing this way and that on the uneven surface. I slid into third, only the ground was so slippery I kept right on sliding into the fence. I was out!

We kept on playing until our toes and fingers were aching from the cold, then we all went to my house. My mother made us hot chocolate and biscuits smothered with butter and jelly. They were the old fashioned southern style biscuits, made with lard, flaky and sweet. She served them right out of the oven. When you cut them open, you saw steam rising from the center. As we ate, we talked about what the Tigers were going to do when the season started in the Spring.

When I wasn't playing sports, I was reading about it in the paper or watching it on TV. Getting to watch a game on the television wasn't a problem when my dad was at home, because he loved baseball as much as me. Maybe more. But when he was out working, which was often, I had to fight for TV time with my brother Albert, who didn't like sports as much as he liked girls and dancing.

We had the one black and white TV in the living room. When he knew there was a baseball game on, Albert would try and take over the television set. June would want to watch a dance party or a movie, or maybe a western. He'd sit right in front of the TV and keep me from reaching the dial. June was the oldest, and he was bigger and stronger than me, though I put up a good fight to get to see my game. Luther sometimes sided with me, because he liked sports, too, and sometimes he sided with June.

One time when my dad wasn't home I insisted it was my turn to pick the show, and I had the ball game on. Albert sneaked down to the basement, pulled the fuse out from the fuse box, and hid it. He figured that I'd get tired of waiting for the electricity to come back on and go outside, and then he could put the fuse back in and watch his dance show or a western.

I went running after him yelling, "June! Gimme back that fuse!"

I stayed in the living room guarding the TV until my dad came home from work. When I told him what June did with the fuse, he got a whipping for messing with the fuse box. Playing around with the fuses could have got him killed, and maybe set the house on fire. My dad didn't put up with us kids doing anything dangerous, like crawling out on the roof over the porch, or being out late at night, or having girls over. When we messed up, he got out the belt, and we learned our lesson.

We all knew that he loved us kids, there was never any doubt about that. It's just that he was a strict sort of parent. He's ex-military, and when he tells you to do something, you know you have to do it or you'll get punished, and there's no talking back or crying your way out of it.

Some of the best times we had were when me and my brothers and my dad watched the ball game together on that old black and white TV. Once in a while, when the money was good, he'd take us to Tiger stadium. Those were exciting days. We would come out of a dark tunnel into the bleacher seats, and the field would be laid out below us greener than any emerald. The white chalk lines were straight and clear, the pitcher's mound was smooth and fresh, and the players in the field in their white uniforms—that would be the home team, since they got to bat last with the home field advantage—they would be throwing the ball around, loose and happy, smiling in the sun. Some-times they'd wave at you when you called their name. That always made us happy.

Baseball was part of our family, part of our daily lives. It was a love we all shared. When I was young and carefree I never could have imagined that baseball, and sports in general, would save my life, but that's exactly what happened.

CHAPTER NINE

Dr. Grifka was telling my family that the odds I would make it were a thousand to one. He said that he expected me to come down with an infection in my open wounds. The infection would enter my bloodstream, and then the bacteria would attack my vital organs. In my weakened condition I wouldn't be able to fight off the bacteria that invaded my body, and the infection would kill me.

Even if an infection didn't kill me, it was even more likely that I would go into shock from losing so much of my blood and fluids. The doctor was pumping in blood and plasma all the time to replace what I was losing, but it was hard to keep up. I needed the blood cells to carry oxygen from my lungs to my organs, and I needed the watery part, the plasma, to carry the protein and antibodies and the nutrients that sustained me. With me having so much of my skin burned away, it looked to Dr. Grifka like it was just a matter of time before I died from shock or infection, or both.

But I didn't know any of that. After the first round of skin grafts I thought I was going to be okay. When you lie in bed at night you don't have much of anything to do but remember things. During the day it was busy, I got treatments and doctor visits and the dressing changes, but at night it was quiet in the ICU and I had a lot of time to think. I thought about baseball.

Just then, I heard the rustle of a newspaper. My dad was turning the page of the sports section of the Detroit News. He looked over at me.

"You awake?" he asked.

"Yeah," I said. My mouth was dry from my losing so much fluid, so I didn't feel like saying a whole lot.

It was three in the morning. I could see the time on a big clock on the wall. My dad was working the three to eleven shift at the Chrysler plant. When his shift was over he came to the hospital to watch over me. He had to get a special pass to stay with me at night. He'd come up to the ICU a little after midnight and sit with me until morning. I'd sleep for an hour or two, then I would wake up in pain. A lot of the time I'd cry out for him, and he'd be there to talk to me and help me hold on until it was time for the next pain shot.

"What you thinking about?" he asked me.

I told him that I was remembering the times when I was a kid,

41

how every morning during the baseball season I'd get up real early in the morning and go to the store to get the early paper so that I could read the box scores. A lot of the times I'd stop at Napoleon's house and wake him up, and I'd drag him out with me to get the paper. Even though he wasn't crazy about sports, he'd still come with me just to be out doing something.

"Remember when Denny McLain won thirty-one games?" I said.

"Course I remember. He's the last pitcher in the Majors to do it." He leaned closer to me. "Remember last year, when Mickey Lolitch beat St. Louis three times in the World Series?"

It was only four months ago that me and my brothers and my dad watched the World Series together on the television. September, 1968. Four months, and a whole other life time ago.

My dad picked up the paper and asked me, "Do you want to hear the sports results?"

I said, "Okay."

He read the reports of the Red Wings, Detroit's professional hockey team. They had a strong team that year, and I was hoping they would win the Stanley Cup. The Red Wings had Gordie Howe, Pete Stemkowski, Garry Unger, and a lot of other powerhouse players. I loved their team leader, Gordie Howe. He and the other forwards were called "The Production Line" after the auto plants.

My dad read the report of the game, then he read all the statistics. We talked about the league and what the Red Wings' chances were. Then he read about Joe Namath, who had quit football and was running a restaurant in New York City. I didn't see what a football quarterback would know about cooking, but maybe his mom taught him when he was young.

After a while I drifted off to sleep. My dad stopped reading out loud. When I woke up he picked up where he left off. It was a lot like when I was a little boy and I'd fall asleep while he was reading me a story. Even though I was confined to a hospital bed, without a TV or radio, I probably knew more about the local sports teams and where they stood than anybody else in Detroit.

My dad was tall and lean. He was a strong man, purposeful in his movements. He didn't waste his words, and he said what he meant without fudging or pretending to be somebody he wasn't. He didn't sweeten his words to make people like him. He spoke his mind, and you either agreed with him or not, it wouldn't change his mind about what he thought. Some might say he was stubborn; I'd say he was strong in his conviction.

Maybe it was because he grew up on a farm. Maybe it was his faith, he was a very devout Christian. But my dad saw a lot of things clearly, and he never wavered in what he believed. When he decided what was the right thing to do in the eyes of the law and in the eyes of God, he went down that path and he never stepped off it.

He fought for his country in the Second World War, serving on a ship in the navy, but he didn't talk about it much. He didn't brag or make a big deal over what he had done, it was just part of his duty. You did what was right and you kept on going without puffing out your chest and telling the world what a big deal you were. That was his way.

He could be strict, but he was always fair. He kept all us kids in line. Sometimes we might have been resentful over the rules, but we knew he did it out of love and wanting us to grow up right. His father, my grandfather Edward McCoy, believed, "Spare the rod, spoil the child." That was how he brought up my dad, and that was how my dad raised us.

He sent us all to church and Sunday school, and we read the Bible at home and prayed regularly. He had us work after school, too, to help put food on the table. When my dad got work delivering news-papers in the morning, all the boys got up at 5 a.m. with him and worked until it was time to go to school.

He taught us to work hard, and to always do what was right, even if it was hard, because he always did things that way. That's my dad.

"Remember when you and your brothers used to help me de-liver the papers?" he asked me, putting the Detroit News down and looking over at me in my hospital bed. "Some mornings it was mighty cold. You'd be near froze to death by the time I got you back home."

"Yup," I said. "I was thinking about that, too."

My mind drifted back to a hard winter morning. Me and my brothers were running along the sidewalks while my dad slowly drove his old '57 Dodge. I was running hard, and the cold air was burning my throat. It was dark. The street lights in my neighborhood reflected off the hard-packed snow. I had a bunch of newspapers tucked under my arm. Each one was folded so that the end was tucked inside the center of the paper and stayed folded. I threw the first paper onto a porch, then I skipped a house and tossed the second one onto another porch.

We had a thousand papers to deliver. My dad would get us boys up, and we sat in the car while he picked up the papers. We had to cover Grand River and Dexter all the way back to Hamilton and Joy Road. It was a huge territory. Dad would drive and we would run alongside and throw the papers onto the porch.

By the time I was halfway through the route my fingers and toes were cold and aching. But the running kept me warm, and besides, it was fun running with my brothers and seeing who would get his bundle of papers out first, my dad calling to us to keep up with him.

Of course, Tony would be lagging behind the rest of us. We would meet up at a corner after finishing a street, and we'd look around.

"Where's Slow?" Luther would say.

"That's him down the street," I said back.

"C'mon!" June would yell to him. "You're holding us up!"

And Slow would trot up to the car. He didn't apologize. He just took his bundle of papers and went right on delivering them. My dad would smile and not bother about it; he would put the car in gear and move on to the next street.

The only part of delivering papers I didn't like was going into the apartment buildings. Although we never had trouble with violence on our block, there were gangs in the surrounding neighborhoods. I had to take the papers into the apartment building and leave them in front of the apartment door. If you left the paper in the front hall it would be stolen, the customer would complain, and I'd get in trouble.

Going through the apartment building always scared me. I'd shake like a leaf whenever I got to that part of the route. Once in a while Napoleon or Preacher would go with me, they knew how scared I was, but most of the time I went alone. I don't think my dad knew how scared I was, but if he did know I believe he would have made me go alone anyway. I had to learn to be strong and stand up for myself.

By the time we finished the paper route we were all hungry and tired out. But we were also proud, because we knew we were helping keep the family going. Everyone had to work, my dad made that plain since we were little, and we didn't mind. We understood that was the way life was, so we better buckle down and do our jobs.

Now I was in the Intensive Care Unit, and I was scared with the same kind of fear I had going into those apartment buildings and worrying about meeting up with a gang. I felt like a little kid again, and, just like when I was young, I needed my dad to take my fear away.

When I woke up from the surgery where they gave me my first skin grafts, my dad was sitting beside the bed watching over me. From that day on through six long, terrible months, as long as I was in the Intensive Care unit, he never missed a single night. He'd work the three to eleven shift in the auto plant, then he would come to the hospital and sit up with me all night. It was like he was on a ship at sea during the war and he volunteered to take the watch at night, only instead of watching out for enemy submarines and enemy planes, he was watching over his son.

If my dad was a strict kind of father, I always felt that was the best kind to have, because he helped me see the right way to be. He and my mom helped steer me away from dangerous ways, like drugs and crime. Because they valued their family so much, I wanted to be a family man early on. Now, here I was, nineteen years of age, with a wife and two daughters of my own. But my extensive injuries made it impossible for me to provide for my family. Instead I needed my mom and dad even more than my baby daughters needed me.

Sometimes, when I lay in my hospital bed remembering all the sports I played my whole life, I'd get discouraged. I didn't think I would ever play those sports again, and they had always been the happiest part of my life. How was I going to get to the Majors and play for the Tigers, or go to work at the auto plant and take care of my family with the kind of burns I had? Would I even make it out of the hospital alive? What would happen to Yvonne and the girls? I didn't know how I was going to be their husband and father if I couldn't provide for them like I always had.

My dad saw that I was getting discouraged.

"Let's say a prayer together, Delbert Ray," he told me.

He opened up his Bible. It was worn and old, he'd had it for so many years. He began to read the 23rd Psalm. "The Lord is my shepherd, I shall not want. He maketh me to lie down in green pastures. He restoreth my soul…"

I mumbled the words under my breath along with him. I couldn't really speak too well, my mouth wouldn't open very wide, with the burns and the bandages. Plus, my lips and throat were so dry, I couldn't drink anything, or even rinse out my mouth, so all in all, I only spoke a few words at a time. But even with that, just saying the prayer silently with my dad made me feel better.

When he was done, my dad said, "You got to be strong, Delbert. You can't give up. Put your faith in the Lord, he'll see you through. The Good Lord has a plan for each one of us. Trust Him and you'll be okay."

"I will, Daddy," I told him. And I did. Or at least, I tried to believe. I put my faith in the Lord. I reached out to my father, who stayed with me every night, and to my mother, who visited me during the day, and I asked God to see me through my terrible ordeal.

I guess you could say I was hoping for a miracle.

CHAPTER TEN

The Detroit Arson Squad and the police were looking for the two men who had started the fire at the Soul Expression. Otto Wandrie was one of the Arson Investigators. He and his team interviewed over a hundred teenagers from the night of the fire. Many of them were admitted to hospitals scattered throughout Detroit. Several of the teens remembered how Kelley and Robinson were angry when they couldn't get back into the club without paying for another ticket. The security guard gave the police a good description of the two suspects.

Mr. Wandrie right away identified the gasoline that was used to start the fire. That part was easy, the gas left chemical traces behind in the ashes. In the vestibule where Delbert and the other teens had been waiting in line, the investigators found the pieces of the charred gas can that Robinson had borrowed from the service station down the street. The can had exploded in the fire.

Once the investigators found the pieces of the gas can, they went around the neighborhood interviewing the gas station attendants. The Marathon station where Robinson borrowed the can in exchange for his onyx ring was only a couple of blocks away, so they got a description of Kelley and Robinson. Within a day of the fire, they were hot on the trail.

Mr. Wandrie and his team inspected the building that housed the Soul Expression. What they found was did not surprise them; it was all too common. The building had not been kept up to the fire codes. There wasn't even a proper exit. The back door opened onto a roof with a broken staircase that was useless. It was a firetrap.

The Dry Cleaners on the first floor was a big factor in the damage, as well. There were chemicals in the shop that ignited, and the burning chemicals sent toxic gases up to the dance floor above. The kids were trapped when the fire broke out. Their only way out was to smash windows and jump from the second floor window at the front of the hall, or drop off of the roof at the back of the building. When they jumped down from the second story, a lot of the kids were hurt.

A few days after the fire, two detectives, Roger Lacasse and Thomas Trueman, came to see me in the ICU. They had photos with them, and they asked me could I look at them? I told the detectives,

"Yes sir, I can see pretty good." My left eye was in good shape. The vision in my right eye was a little fuzzy from being burned, but I could see well enough to look at pictures.

I looked at every one of the photographs, taking my time. There were ten of them. After I got through them, the detectives asked me did I recognize any of them from the Club. Right away, I pointed to one of the photographs. I didn't know his name, but I knew he was one of the guys in the street outside the Soul Expression.

"Are you sure you recognize him?" they said. They wanted to be certain that I recognized the guy, because if I wasn't really sure, my testimony wouldn't hold up when they put him on trial. If I was even a little bit unsure of myself, then the defense lawyer would object, and the jury might let the guy off.

The detectives asked me at least twice, "You're sure this is the man you saw outside the Soul Expression the night of the fire?" I told them I was sure, he had looked right at me and said they were fixing to "do something." It was an expression I will never forget.

The detectives didn't tell me who the guy was, but later I learned that the man I recognized was Eugene Kelley. He was from Chicago. They got a line on him pretty quick. I heard later that somebody at the Soul Expression knew Kelley, so the police started looking for him right away. He had a police record, so they had pictures of him and an address from his previous arrests.

The police didn't know who the second guy was. Yet. They were hoping that when they found Kelley, Kelley would lead them to his partner.

The Detroit newspapers had a story about the fire for two days, because there were so many people hurt in the fire. There were over 60 people injured, with me being the worst of them. They spelled my name wrong, but they described the fire and the injuries very well.

After the detectives left, I lay back in my bed and hoped that they found the two guys soon. It wasn't that I was filled with anger or hatred for them. But I wanted justice to be done, a lot of kids were hurt. A man who would set a building on fire that was filled with innocent kids should be put behind bars and kept there the rest of his life.

Officers Lacasse and Trueman got Kelley's name from the getaway driver, Theodore Wallace. They picked up Wallace five days after the fire, based on testimony from witnesses at the Soul Expres-

sion who described the getaway car. *Once they found him, Wallace told the Detectives about Eugene Kelley. He also told them about his two Detroit friends, Donald Jones and Ulysses Butts, who were with him in the car that night. Wallace said that he and his two friends didn't have anything to do with setting the fire, they were just along for the ride.*

All three of the men from Detroit – Wallace, Jones and Butts - were charged with crimes related to the arson. When the charges were brought before the judge in Recorders court, the judge dismissed the charges against Jones and Butts. He ruled that those two had had nothing to do with setting the fire, they were only bystanders. They hadn't done anything to try and stop Kelley and Robinson, and they didn't call the police and hand them in, but that wasn't a crime, so they were let go.

Theodore Wallace, the getaway driver, didn't get off so easily. The judge refused to throw out the charges against him, and he scheduled Wallace to go to trial. After the charges were made against Wallace, the District Attorney began to put pressure on Wallace to cooperate. He told Wallace how bad it would be for him if he went to trial and was found guilty. So many people were badly hurt, the charges could go all the way to attempted murder, not to mention the terrible injuries that a lot of us suffered from the fire. There was also the fact that they had burned down a whole building.

Wallace was facing serious charges. He knew he could get a long prison term. Wallace was young, he was looking at his future, and he didn't want to spend half his life in prison.

So the negotiations between the District Attorney and Wallace's lawyer began. If Wallace would agree to testify against the other two, the ones who set the fire, and if he admitted he was guilty of helping them, the DA would charge him with a lesser crime. He would face a sentence that did not demand a long prison term. If Wallace refused to cooperate, he could be put away for the rest of his life.

Even while the Arson squad and the Detroit police were anxious to find the ones who started the fire, I was worried about the little baby across from me who was burned. I heard her crying every day. Sometimes she'd wake me up. Her cry cut through my heart just as much as the pain of the dressing changes cut through my body.

Marlene told me the baby had been burned, but she couldn't

tell me what happened. That was confidential information, she explained. The baby's mom came every day to hold her and take care of her. She was a young black woman, not too tall, sort of thin. I wasn't able to talk to her, but I did ask Marlene every day how the baby was doing.

"She's coming along okay, Delbert," she would tell me. Every day she reassured me that the baby was coming along. I got so that I didn't want to start my therapy or do anything else until I got word on the baby's condition. I felt so bad that this little person had to go through the same kind of torture that I had. She didn't understand what happened to her or why she was suffering, At least I could deal with it. I had my family praying with me and the doctors explaining things to me.

But the baby had nothing like that. All she had was her pain, and it hurt me every time she cried out. I wished that there was something I could do to make things easier for her and for her mother, but I was stuck in my bed, I couldn't get up and walk over to her to try and comfort her in some way.

The fire had turned *me* into a helpless little baby. I couldn't do anything for myself. The old Delbert who held two jobs and played sports and went out to parties was gone. So was the young father who held his baby daughters on his lap. The old life I once knew was turned to ashes; the ashes were being blown scattered by the cold Michigan winds.

But I didn't understand any of that at the time. All I knew was that I was in pain, that the doctors and nurses were doing everything they could to help me, and that my family and friends were behind me one-hundred per cent.

All I could do was pray and hope for the best, listen to my dad read to me at night, and take my treatments during the day.

CHAPTER ELEVEN

That first week in the Intensive Care Unit the morphine kept me in a dreamy state a lot of the time. I'd wake up suddenly with pain shooting up my legs and arms. The nurse would get the morphine and inject it into my bloodstream through the intravenous tubing, and after a while the pain would ease off some, although it never left me entirely.

Dr. Grifka and the other doctors changed my bandages twice a day. Even with the morphine, the pain was excruciating. The doctor had a regular schedule, and once I learned what it was I began to watch the clock. I'd wake up early, feeling pretty good. I'd be comfortable, not in too much pain. If I could just lie still and not be moved, I'd be okay.

But then, as the clock on the wall ran around, it got closer and closer to nine in the morning, and that was when Dr. Grifka would change the dressings. I came to fear that time. As the hand on the clock slowly went around, I'd start to sweat. I'd feel my heart pounding in my chest. The fear would come over me, and it was a powerful fear. Knowing the pain was coming was as bad as the dressing change itself. By the time the clock came around to nine, I was shaking with fear. I was terrified.

Dr. Grifka would come in and talk to me real nice. He was encouraging. He put his hand on my forehead, like a kindly priest, and he waited for Marlene to give me the morphine. Then he and his assistants would start with my legs, and I would start to cry out, "Daddy! Daddy!"

They would go up my legs to my hips. There were open wounds on my abdomen and lower chest. My upper chest wasn't quite as bad, but my arms were burned down to the bone. A lot of the muscle was burned off, like I'd been roasted on a spit and somebody forgot to take me off when I was done.

It's hard to say what part of the dressing change was the worst, but if I had to choose one, I'd probably say it was when they changed the dressings on my hands. Dr. Grifka wanted to wrap my fingers separately. He knew that if he left them wrapped together, they would heal in a locked fist. The fingers would grow together and end up like a plastic toy soldier that you put over a candle and half-melt down, making its arms and legs fuse together in a lump.

But the pain of wrapping my fingers individually was too excruciating, even with the morphine. If the doctor even touched one of my fingers and tried to separate it from the others, the pain made me scream and want to leap off the bed. In the end, he was forced to wrap my hand in a closed fist and let the fingers fuse to each other.

After Dr. Grifka finished with the dressing change, it would take me an hour or longer to settle down. The pain kept running through me, like the ringing in your ears after you hear an explosion. In the afternoon, around four, Dr. Grifka would come back and have to do it all over again.

I went to surgery on the average of twice a week for the first few months. When one of the skin grafts was two or three weeks old, my body would reject it, and Dr. Grifka would remove it. Then he would place a new graft on. I needed them everywhere. I was still leaking a lot of blood and plasma into my bandages, although the loss was slowed down quite a bit by the grafts.

By this time some of my skin was healed enough that I could donate skin from one part of my body to cover another part that wasn't healed. That's how most skin grafts are done. When I needed still more skin, Dr. Grifka began calling hospitals around the country, asking did they have somebody who had just died or who was about to die, and could they harvest some of that person's skin?

Between the cadaver donors and my own skin, the doctors didn't have to ask my family to donate any more. They still donated blood, along with the auto workers in the UAW. My family and my friends donated blood the whole time I was in Detroit General, and every one of their pints was credited to my account with the Red Cross.

I didn't know it until a long time later, but Dr. Grifka had my name on waiting lists for skin donors in half the states around the country. He told the doctors in the other hospitals how sick I was, but also what a remarkable survivor I was. He said to the doctors in other states that he was going to keep treating me until my skin was completely closed, whatever it cost. My name must have been known from New York half way to California.

Planes flew in to Detroit Airport from all over the country, and the donated skin was carried by ambulance to Detroit General Hospital. In the hospital, they took me to the Operating Room week after week, and they kept patching me up, removing old grafts that were ready to slough off, and placing new ones on. The places that were still open and leaking and didn't get a graft were covered in silver nitrate and wet gauze.

With all of the operations and phone calls and pleading for grafts, Dr. Grifka and his team saved my life. If he hadn't worked so hard for me, I would be just a photograph on my parent's mantle and a memory, instead of a living man. My daughters would be growing up without their father. But with the care of the doctors and the nurses and the grace of God, I survived.

The days turned over, like innings in a ball game. I'd wake up and see Marlene, with her warm smile. When she came to check on me, one of the first things I asked was how was the baby was doing? Marlene always told me the baby was doing fine, and not to worry about her. That made me feel a lot better, knowing the baby was going to make it home.

I was about as weak as a baby myself. I could just lift my arms up off the bed a few inches, but not much more. Before the fire I'd been a pretty good athlete, fast on my feet, swinging a pretty good bat. Now I couldn't even open my mouth more than a crack. The muscles in my jaw were tight, my lips were dried and peeling, and I didn't seem to have a lot of wind. I could say a few words, but I got tired quickly.

I couldn't eat or drink anything. Between not getting any food inside me and losing all the fluids from my burns, I was losing weight fast. The nurses weighed me every morning. They had a hammock that they put under me and lifted me up in it. They weighed me just like a fish on a fish scale, hanging in the air above my bed. It was scary hanging there, but the nurses assured me they had never dropped a patient. I was still scared of the scale.

I got down to fifty-seven pounds. Not that I was ever a big guy, but that weight wasn't healthy. Anybody could see losing so much weight was dangerous, but nobody knew how to make it stop.

My body was so sensitive to pressure, it hurt a lot when the weighed me, even though they were as gentle as they could be. The hammock pinched me in the arms and legs. It didn't hurt as much as the dressing change, but still, it was very painful. I used to dread when they came to my bed early in the morning with the weighing scale. It wasn't just the hanging in the air that I hated; I dreaded seeing the numbers on the scale go down day after day as my body wasted away.

Once Dr. Grifka knew that the first round of skin grafts were sticking, he started sending me for dressing changes in a big steel tub. It looked a lot like an old-fashioned bathtub, only it was made out of stainless steel. It was better to put me in the tank, because the water loosened the bandages, which got sticky from the dried blood and fluid and were hard to pull off. If the doctors pulled them when they were sticky, they might dislodge the skin grafts, too.

Even if they didn't loosen the grafts, pulling a sticky dressing off of a wound caused terrible pain, and it always started me bleeding. By putting my whole body in the tub of water, the doctors could loosen the dressings and pull them away safely without my losing quite as much blood.

My dad came with me the first time they took me to the tank. When they wheeled me over to the tank on a stretcher, I watched Marlene as she poured salt from a Morton's salt container into the water, and I knew I was in for it. They put salt into the water in order to kill the bacteria that grows on the skin, just like the way they salt fish to preserve them. Marlene and Dr. Grifka picked me up on a sheet and lowered me into the water. It wasn't hard for them to lift me, I was so skinny.

As my body settled into the water, my skin felt like I was being burned all over again. I had open wounds all over my body, and salt in a wound causes a terrible burning pain. I gritted my teeth and tried not to cry out, but sometimes I couldn't help myself, my skin felt like it was on fire.

"Daddy! Daddy!" I cried out.

My dad told me, "Be strong, Delray, those are healing waters. They're going to make you well."

As soon as I was lowered into the tank, blood poured out into the water. The blood formed a red cloud that spread until the whole tub was turned crimson. It was terrible to see. It looked like I was bleeding out of control into the water.

The doctor started to unwrap the dressings and peel them away from my body. When the burns were exposed to the salty water, they leaked even *more* blood. Once he had all of the dressings off, he took me out of the water and put me back on the stretcher on a clean sheet.

After they patted my skin dry, they spread silver nitrate solution on the burns. That stung almost as much as the salt water did. The doctor explained that I needed the silver nitrate because it killed the bacteria that was always growing on my skin.

Finally, the doctor wrapped fresh bandages all over me, from my feet and ankles all the way up my legs. My hips, buttocks and chest, my arms and even my face were wrapped in dry bandages. Only my privates and my eyes and mouth were left exposed.

The trips to the tank and the bleeding into the water were too much for my mom. She couldn't stand to see it. She started to visit me less often. My dad was in every major battle in the Pacific except Pearl Harbor. He was in the Atlantic bringing supplies to England when the Japanese bombed Pearl Harbor. The captain turned the boat around and headed back to the U.S. as fast as he could go. With all his experiences in the war, my dad was tougher than my mom, so he was able to stay with me when I first went for my dressing changes in the tank.

Lying on the stretcher with the dressings off, I had the first look at my body. It was a terrible sight. My left hand and arm looked like the muscle had been completely stripped away. There was hardly anything left, just some flaps of skin over bones. My legs were half stripped of muscle, too. I looked like a carcass in a slaughterhouse, not a man.

The salt water left my wounds clean and moist. I understood I needed the treatments to keep me from contracting an infection, but it was so painful, I didn't want to go back for another the following day.

"Do I have to go back tomorrow?" I asked the doctor, scared of facing that terrible burning all over again. Dr. Grifka told me, yes, I had to go to the tank every day.

My dad told me he would stay with me, and he spent as much time with me in the hospital as he could. I don't know how much sleep he got, but it couldn't have been much more than 4 hours a day. But he was strong. He was raised on a farm in a poor family where you worked from sun up to sun down and then worked some more. Because he grew up on a farm and had been in the war, he was tough. He was determined to fight until the battle was won; that meant I was going to have to fight alongside him.

"Those are healing waters," he told me again. "You got to go every day. You just got to." He promised to go with me to the treatments, even though he really should have gone home and got some sleep. But he didn't even look tired. Or discouraged. He was always sure I was getting better every day.

My mom was too upset, seeing me so hurt and in so much pain. She wanted to be with me, but it hurt her too much to see what I was going through. It hurt me, too, seeing my mom in pain, so a part of me was glad she stayed away.

My mother wasn't the only one who couldn't look at me in my

condition. When my wife Yvonne first came to visit she looked like she was in shock. She could hardly stand to see me. Like my mom, she was broken up, seeing me so badly burned. As the days dragged on, she visited me less and less often.

A part of me understood that it was scary for Yvonne to see me so torn up and bleeding and close to death. She was seventeen, just a kid. She wasn't used to dealing with frightening things like this. She wasn't a nurse, trained to handle sick people every day. My injuries and my being so close to death were too much for her.

Even though I understood why my wife didn't want to come see me too often, another part of me needed her to visit me every day. I needed to hear how the girls were doing. I needed to know that she was still my wife and that she would be with me forever. I was as helpless as the baby across from me who cried in the night. That baby had her mom coming in every day to hold her and comfort her. I had my dad and my brothers and sisters and friends, and that was great for my morale. But I needed my wife with me, too.

Every time she came to see me, Yvonne acted like she needed to run out of the ICU. She looked like she was as scared as the kids in the Soul Expression were when they ran from the fire and jumped out of the window. I understood she was scared, but I needed her badly; I felt lost without her. It killed me to see her turn and leave after just a few minutes at my side.

I only hoped that she wasn't thinking of jumping out of our marriage, too.

I was burning up. The sweat was running down my face and chest. The unmerciful sun, stuck in a clear blue North Carolina sky, was hot and strong as me and my brothers picked tobacco on my grandfather McCoy's farm.

The farm was in a sleepy little town called Silverdale. Silverdale is about twenty miles from Camp Lejune, but it isn't even on the map, it's so small. While me and my brothers were at Grandpa McCoy's place, my sisters were with my mother visiting her family, the McDonalds, over in Maysville, another sleepy little farm town.

They have a lot of little towns like Silverdale and Maysville down south. They're nothing more than a crossroads and a general store, with farms spread out in the surrounding hills. If you blink twice when you drive through, you'll miss the whole town and never even know it was there.

Our family didn't just farm in North Carolina. Back up north in Detroit, most of my friends called us McCoy brothers "The Farmers", because my dad always had us digging in the back yard. He had us planting vegetables. For a while we even had chickens in our yard in a little hutch. I guess it was because my mom and dad both grew up on farms in North Carolina, not far from each other. When they moved to Detroit, they kept right on planting and growing.

We were just like real farmers, too. In the warm weather when one of our friends came by, my dad would put him right to work digging. Napoleon had to sneak up to the yard and try and catch me before my dad saw him, because as soon as he got a look at Nate, my dad put him to work.

The food we grew helped us through many a summer and fall, and even through the winter. My mom put up fruits and vegetables in jars—tomatoes, cucumbers, carrots and greens. We had greens all winter from our garden.

When my dad was laid off from the auto plant, he made money any way he could, delivering newspapers, magazines, or phone books. He'd take any job that would pay the bills and put food on the table, and the vegetables from the garden were a blessing when things were tight.

In the summer, my dad brought me and my brothers down to his father's farm. We helped our grandparents, Edward and Sula

McCoy, with the chores. By the time we started going down to Silverdale to help, all of my grandparents' children except for their daughter, Christobel, had grown up and moved on, so we were really important to him. We were "The Farmers."

They lived in a little one-story wooden farmhouse on maybe ten acres of land. There was a barn, a chicken coop, and a pigsty. They didn't have any plumbing in the house, so you went out back to the outhouse to do what you had to do.

For water we went to the pump outside by the back porch and worked the handle. We'd carry the water inside for cooking. To bathe we'd bring in several bucket, heat the water on the wood stove, and wash standing up, kind of like they wash you in the hospital. Once in a while we'd get a good rain, and my grandfather would collect rainwater in a barrel, but most of the time we had to use the well for our water.

Grandfather McCoy would wake all us kids up at six every morning. "Time to work, boys," he would say, coming into our room and putting on the light. "Time to work!"

He was a good-sized man, six feet tall and solidly built. He had a natural dark complexion, which was made even darker from working out in the sun all the time, and he was serious. Like my dad, he meant business. You did what he told you, or you got a licking.

Sometimes, when we finished the chores that grandfather gave us, we'd try to duck away before he saw us because we knew he always had another job for us to do. There was never any end to work on a farm, grandfather made that clear.

You might think that I hated going down to Silverdale every summer and working so hard, but I didn't. Even though I worked hard, I had a great time on the farm. I had June and Ball and Slow with me. A lot of the time, we had cousins staying on the farm, too, and that made it even more fun. The farm was a great place to leave the kids; it was our own special summer camp.

One of the hardest jobs was picking tobacco. I didn't mind picking tobacco, even though it was hard work, because I was strong, even if I wasn't a big husky kid. We picked the tobacco in bunches, called sand lugs. They were sandy, because they grew in sandy soil, and lugs was the name for the crop when it was green. You'd tie the lugs in a bunch and drop them in a little cart we rolled between the rows of tobacco plants.

Once the cart was full of tobacco leaves, we'd take it to the barn. There we'd hang the lugs high up from the rafters to cure. Sitting on the dirt floor of the barn was a big brick oven my grandfather had built. He'd load the oven with wood and get it roaring, then he'd close the barn doors. This was in the middle of the summer in North Carolina, don't forget. Inside the barn, the air would get hot and dry, a hundred and fifty degrees. That would speed up the curing process. It usually took about five or six days to dry out the tobacco and turn it golden, with the fire burning the whole time.

I loved the smell of the drying tobacco. Some kids might be tempted to take some of that fresh tobacco and smoke it themselves, but we never did. Partly, that was because my grandfather was just like my dad. *Strict.* He would have given us a good whupping if he caught us smoking. But that wasn't the only reason we didn't try it. We just didn't see the point. Smoking didn't seem grown up or fun to us, so we left it alone.

We had other chores to do, like weeding the vegetable patch or fixing the old wooden fences that kept the animals from getting out. The good thing about working in the garden was we could see the vegetables and fruits getting riper and riper every day. By the end of our stay the watermelon would be huge. We'd cut big slices and sit out on the porch eating the fruit and spitting out the seeds. Being boys, we naturally had to see who could spit the seeds the farthest. Since we were in the country, my grandfather didn't punish us for spitting seeds, which we would never get away with up North.

Feeding the pigs was the one chore I really hated to do, because I was scared of them. I was only ten or eleven. My older brothers weren't afraid of them, and my youngest brother, Tony, wasn't scared either. Slow always loved animals. He liked dogs, cats, birds, rabbits—all sorts of animals. He usually had some pet in the back yard. One time he and his friend, Ricky Reno, had a little brown rabbit they named Bosco, after the chocolate syrup. He loved that rabbit so much, he would spend all day Saturday with it, feeding it and talking to it and playing with it.

I was especially scared of the oldest pig. He was mean, and he'd chase me all over the yard. A couple of times he got out of his pen and chased me. My brothers laughed at me and didn't try to help catch him at all. In the end my grandfather would catch the pig, and then he would scold us all for letting him get free.

They had two mules on the farm. Of the two, the one they called Ned was the more stubborn one. He was old and tired and worn out. Ned had worked on the logging company's land, dragging fresh cut trees out of the forest. When he got too old and tired to pull the logs, they sold him at auction, which is where my grandfather got him.

One time, June dared me to get on Ned's back and ride him. We loved the cowboys and Indian shows, so it was only natural that I'd want to ride the mule, just like the Cisco Kid. I got on Ned, with no saddle, nothing to hang on to but the halter he had on his head. That mule was old and tired, but he had more meanness in him than he had tiredness. He bucked me off right away, then he came after me with his teeth bared, ready to bite me. That was the one time that June and Ball came to my rescue. They grabbed Ned by the halter and got him away from me. I never tried to ride any mule ever again.

For me, the worst part of working on the farm was killing the chickens. You killed them by wringing their neck. You would grab the chicken by the throat, flip him over and break his neck. That was scary for me, and I hated to do it, so my grandfather mainly left that job for June or Luther. Nothing bothered Luther, Ball wasn't scared of anything, so he usually ended up doing the slaughtering.

Us kids didn't have anything to do with slaughtering the pigs, but grandfather showed us how he did it. The pig would be in the mud pit. He would shoot the pig in the head, then he'd cut his throat. I was afraid of the pigs, so I tried to stick with picking the tobacco and the vegetables. I could never get used to killing the chickens or the pigs.

The summer days were long and hot, the evenings were cool and peaceful. Even though we worked harder than our dad made us do up north, harder even than running behind the car delivering newspapers, my brothers and I were never happier. We were four brothers together, we had our cousins with us, and we had the countryside for our playground.

If we could just get done with our chores and get away before grandfather called us all back to work.

CHAPTER THIRTEEN

A couple of weeks after I was admitted to the Intensive Care Unit I started having fevers and chills. With all the fluid that was constantly leaking out of my burned skin, I was getting more and more dehydrated.

I was thirsty all the time. My lips and my tongue were dry as sandpaper. Even with the transfusions and the other intravenous fluids the nurses gave me, I still felt like I was stranded in a desert without any water. Next to the pain, the thing that bothered me most was that I wasn't allowed to eat or drink anything.

Right next to my bed was a sink. The nurses and doctors and orderlies went there a hundred times a day to wash their hands. Even the visitors used that sink. Sometimes they'd take a cup of water from the tap and drink it right in front of me. They'd even cup their hands under the running water and drink like they were at a running stream. I could hear them sucking up the water, and it drove me crazy.

They didn't mean anything by it, I understood that, but seeing them drink the water would tear me up. I'd ask my mom, "Mama, get me some water. Please get me a little water." But Dr. Grifka wouldn't let her give me anything. It was torture. The only thing she was allowed to do was to wet a washrag and touch my lips with it. But I couldn't drink anything, and my thirst was making me crazy.

I couldn't open my mouth to drink properly, anyway. The skin around my mouth had contracted, and I could only open my mouth a crack. I went for weeks without anything going into my mouth. My mother holding the wet washcloth to my lips was the only relief I was allowed for my thirst.

Being dehydrated made me weak, because I needed fluid to move the blood through my veins. I was still losing weight, too. I'd never been fat, but soon my weight was dropping off me. The doctors were only giving me intravenous nutrition: sugar and water, basically. As a result, I was losing weight and feeling dry all the time.

My temperature went higher and higher, and that made my thirst get worse and worse. My lips were cracked from being so dry, my tongue was scratchy in my mouth. I couldn't even make my spit properly, I was so dried out.

I begged and begged Marlene to give me a drink of water. She asked Dr. Grifka if I could have some ice chips to wet my mouth. He said that was okay, so she brought a cup of ice and a spoon. The skin was so tight around my mouth, Marlene had to pry it open with a tongue blade just to be able to slip a piece of ice into my mouth. It was painful, but I was willing to take it just to have something that would relieve my terrible thirst.

Now, a couple of chips of ice might not sound like much to most people, but to me it was pure relief. The cold ice on my tongue was soothing. I rolled the piece around my mouth until it was all melted, and then I swallowed the little bit of water down. It was wonderful! Better than a cold beer.

I couldn't have a whole lot of ice. Marlene spaced it out all through her shift, like little rewards. The ice gave me something good to look forward to. I was happy knowing there was more of it coming, if I just held out.

Even with the ice chips, my fever got worse. That night, while my dad was sitting watching over me, I started to get the shivers from the high temperature. I was shaking so hard that the rails on the side of the bed were rattling. Dr. Grifka said I had an infection. They were giving me an antibiotic. Penicillin. I felt weak and hot and was in a lot of pain.

My dad told me what happened next. The alarm went off on the heart monitor over my bed, and before he knew what was happening, a pack of doctors and nurses came running to my bed. He said that it looked just like a stampede of horses. They came running in through the doors from both sides of the ICU, calling out orders and grabbing pieces of equipment.

As my dad backed away into a corner to be out of the way, one of the doctors put the paddles on my chest and sent an electric shock through my heart, which had stopped beating. My body arched off of the bed. The doctor pumped a lot of drugs into my veins, and after a couple of minutes, they brought me back to life.

My dad stood in the corner out of the way and watched the whole thing. He didn't know how he was going to be able to call my mom and tell her the bad news if I didn't make it. It was a great relief for him when the doctor came and told him that they had me stabilized again.

Dr. Grifka told him later that my blood pressure got very low because of the infection and the dehydration. He said he didn't know if my heart would keep going from the strain; that I might have another arrest at any time, but for now, I was stable.

When the doctors left, my dad sat down again beside me, though I was in a deep sleep from the arrest, and watched over me until morning. Then he went home to get some rest. He came back to see me that afternoon. He didn't go to work that day because he was so worried about me, my heart having stopped.

My dad came to my bedside in the afternoon and looked down at me. "How you feeling?" he asked.

"Pretty good," I told him. I looked up into my father's worried face. "I had a vision last night," I told him.

"Is that right?" he said.

"Uh-huh." I told him I saw something that was so real, I felt like it really happened. Maybe it had been a dream, but it seemed so real.

In the vision, I was sitting by a pond. My feet were bare and in the water, and I wasn't burned at all; I was completely healed. There was a bright light in the sky above me, like when I used to pick tobacco on Grandfather McCoy's farm. Even though the light was very strong, it didn't hurt my eyes. In fact, it was comforting. Soothing, even.

I looked up, and I saw a single cloud in the sky. The cloud formed an image, like a man's face. It was blurry and indistinct, but still, it looked like a face. A voice from the cloud spoke to me. It was a deep voice, and it spoke softly to me.

The voice told me, "Pick the watermelon from the vine and suck the juice." The voice told me that quite clearly. At the time I knew exactly what the voice meant. It wasn't strange to me at all, it made perfect sense. The voice was calling me to go to Heaven, and that was okay with me. My body was healed in heaven, and I wanted to be made whole and have my pain taken away. I was ready to go.

When I told my dad about the vision, he went right to Dr. Grifka and asked him if it would be okay for me to drink some watermelon juice. I don't know if he thought that what I saw was from God, or if it was just a dream, but my dad was sure that it was something that would help me get well. He believed what the vision had told me.

Dr. Grifka wasn't sure I could handle food yet, even something light, like fruit juice. My dad told the doctor that they had been giving me the ice chips, and I'd swallowed them down without any problems, so why not give me some juice as well? The doctor thought it was worth a try. I'd get more water into me, which I always needed, plus there'd be vitamins in the juice.

My dad came back and told me that Dr. Grifka gave him the

okay to feed me watermelon juice. "But," he said, "there's a problem. I don't know where I'm gonna get the watermelon in February, it's the middle of the winter. In Michigan."

I told him, "Call down to grandpa's farm in Silverdale. He'll have plenty of watermelon."

I wasn't thinking very clearly. Marlene was giving me morphine every day, and that morphine can cloud your mind. On top of that, when you suffer a cardiac arrest, your brain doesn't get very much oxygen while the heart is stopped. Even though the doctors got my heart started very quickly, I still suffered a little bit of damage to my brain, and that probably made my thinking even fuzzier than the morphine did.

I didn't think about the fact that, by the middle of the winter, all the fruit from the farm would have been eaten or sold by now. There was no way that my dad could find fresh watermelon at that time of year. I only knew that I *had* to have the juice from the fruit. The voice had told me to drink it, and I believed that I would never recover from my burns unless I had that watermelon.

My dad went home and called down to North Carolina, just to see if they had any watermelon left over from the summer, but of course, they didn't. So he went around to the grocery stores all over Detroit. He talked to the produce men in the markets. He searched all over the city. Finally, after searching for several days, he found a produce man in a Fruit and Vegetable Market who had a single watermelon kept in cold storage. It wasn't as sweet as when it was fresh picked, but it was still good. My dad bought that big old watermelon and brought it to the hospital.

When I saw him coming across the ICU and up to my bed with the watermelon in his hands, my heart felt like it swelled up, but it wasn't swelling with pain or sickness, it was swelling with joy.

I said to my dad, "You see? I told you grandpa McCoy would have some watermelon for me. You got that from grandpa's farm in North Carolina, didn't you?"

"That's right, Delray," he told me. "This watermelon is from your grandfather's farm in North Carolina, flown up here special, just for you."

I believed that the watermelon had special healing powers. I couldn't wait to drink it. Marlene cut the watermelon into slices and squeezed the juice into a cup. She got a training cup with a mouthpiece from the children's ward. I didn't have the use of my hands, which had been so badly burned that I couldn't bend the fingers to hold a cup. The muscles had been burned down to the bones, and what was left had frozen into a clenched fist.

I couldn't even bend my arm to bring my hand to my mouth, so the nurse had to hold it for me. She held the cup with the mouth-piece up to my lips with one hand, and she propped up my head with the other. Her hands were gentle and firm. She smiled at me as if it were my birthday and I was taking a big bite out of my birthday cake.

I could only take a little sip at a time. I let the juice roll around in my mouth. I tasted it every kind of way you can taste something. On my tongue, under my tongue, across my lips, in the back of my throat. I tasted and tasted that juice, and it was even better than the ice chips! It was glorious! It was Heaven-sent.

I sucked on the cup like a little baby, and I ran my tongue over my moist lips. I let the juice roll down my throat and into my stomach. I could feel the healing power of that watermelon juice as soon as it got inside me. I was so happy I was smiling and feeling stronger and stronger. I was going to get better. I was going to make it!

Looking back, I suppose that it was more the power of suggestion that healed me than the juice of that old watermelon, kept in a cold storage for five months. But my soul needed nourishment as much as my body did, and faith was the nutrient that kept my soul alive. Without that faith I would have given up and let myself die, I'm sure of it. I couldn't have kept on fighting day after day, with all the pain of the dressing changes and the losing weight and the bleeding into the tank.

If I didn't have the hope that came from my dad bringing me the watermelon, and if I didn't believe in its healing powers, I would have given up and quit. If I didn't have my family behind me every day, and nurses like Marlene and doctors like Dr. Grifka encouraging me and working with me, I would have just reached for Heaven where my body was healed and whole. I would be dead, and my suffering would be over.

I believed in the words of the vision. I believed in the healing powers of the juice from the watermelon. Most of all, I believed in the strength of my family and my faith, and in the skills and dedication of my nurses and doctors.

It wasn't until quite recently that I learned where my father really found that watermelon. That it came from a local Fruit and Vegetable Market right outside of Detroit, and not my grandfather's farm in North Carolina. I wasn't upset to learn the truth. He was right to tell me that little lie, because on that day I started growing stronger and putting on weight. I didn't even have any more fevers.

After suffering my cardiac arrest, and the first bunch of skin grafts, and the treatments in the saltwater tub, there was one funny moment that got all of us laughing, even Marlene and Dr. Grifka. About a month after the fire, I got a notice from the draft board. They ordered me to report for basic training. They drafted me! I wished I could have gone. I was willing to go to Viet Nam and take my chances if it would cure my burns.

I would love to be able to get out of my hospital bed and march right on down to the recruiting office and sign up, but my hands were bandaged and I couldn't use my fingers. My legs were wrapped in bandages and I couldn't walk. My eyesight was fuzzy, so I couldn't see too good, but I'd have put on the uniform and saluted any officer that came my way if it would have meant not having to go through the pain of the dressing changes day after day.

CHAPTER FOURTEEN

When I was thirteen or fourteen I wanted to do things that I saw the older guys doing, and a lot of older guys liked to gamble. They played craps and poker, and they bet on the horses. It was a way to have fun and cut up with your friends.

There was an older guy who lived in the neighborhood named Johnny. Johnny was always trying to get us over to his house to play cards. We were young and foolish, and we looked up to Johnny like he was a big brother. We didn't understand that he wasn't a positive influence.

Johnny gave us wine to drink. That made us feel we were really grown up. My dad would have got the strap out and tanned our hides if we ever got caught drinking. Johnny gambled and drank and had women over. We thought he was cool, so we'd go over there and he'd get us playing cards.

This one time we were at Johnny's, he brought out a bag of marijuana and rolled a cigarette. He had the papers and the bag of weed, and he rolled a joint and lit it. He took a deep breath in and held it there, showing us how it was done. Then, when he let out his breath, he smiled and passed it on to Nate.

Napoleon took a breath just like Johnny had done, and while he was holding his breath, he handed it to me. I felt funny taking it, I knew it was something I shouldn't be doing. But I wanted to know what it was like. People talked about getting high a lot, it was the sixties. I took my turn, and pretty soon we finished the whole joint.

That was when I got sick. My stomach felt like it was turned inside out. I got dizzy and couldn't walk right. I stumbled out of Johnny's house and threw up right in front of his house. Johnny yelled after me, "Don't throw up in front of my house, go down the street!"

I staggered down the street like I was drunk. I felt terrible. Every block or two I'd have to stop and throw up again. By the time I was halfway home I was heaving up acid; there wasn't any food left in my stomach. Nate kept a hand on my arm and helped me stay on course.

I was sick for two whole days. My parents never knew, which was a good thing, because my daddy would have whooped me till I was crying for mercy if he ever found out I'd tried marijuana. After that I vowed I would never use any kind of drugs again. I figured that if marijuana made me so sick, harder drugs like heroin would mess my body up permanent.

Besides, I wanted to be a professional baseball player more than anything in the world. I knew that if I messed around with drugs and ruined my body I'd never be able to try out for a place with the Detroit Tigers. I'd never get to play alongside Willie Horton and Mickey Lolitch. So I made a decision to never use drugs ever again.

Even though we didn't smoke marijuana any more, we still drank beer that Johnny bought for us. We didn't think of beer as a drug. One day we were playing cards at Johnny's for quarters, nickels and dimes. Napoleon and Tony were doing the gambling, while I mainly watched them. I didn't have any money to put in for chips, so I went home.

After a while, Nate won eight dollars from Johnny. Tony had lost, so Johnny sent him out. Right after that, Johnny locked the door on Nate. He wasn't going to let him go until he had his money back.

Tony came running home and told me what was happening. I ran over to Johnny's house. The door was locked, there was no way for me to get in. I yelled through the door, "Nate, you all right?"

He yelled back, "I'm okay, I'm okay!"

I was scared he *wasn't* okay. That Johnny was making him say he was okay when he was really in trouble. I pictured Johnny holding a knife on Nate, or maybe even a gun.

I found a red brick out on the front walk. I threw that brick right into the front window. It smashed real loud. I wanted Johnny to think that somebody was breaking into his house. I ran around to the back and called through the back door, "Nate, come on out. Nate!"

As soon as Nate heard the glass breaking, he figured it had to be me trying to help him. He ran to the back door and unlocked it. I pulled the door open, and Nate came running out. We ran as fast as we could through the alley and back to our neighborhood. We kept looking behind us to see if Johnny was following, but he couldn't do anything to us out in the street. After all, it wasn't like Nate was stealing money from him. He was only stealing himself.

We stayed away from Johnny's after that, and stuck to our friends. It was a lot safer, and I didn't end up throwing up or running for my life.

Growing up in Detroit in the 1960's meant that I came up with a lot of great music. We listened to the new groups coming out of Motown, like The Shirelles, The Temptations, The Marvellettes, and many more.

We went to high school during the week, and we couldn't wait for the weekend so that we could buy the latest single from one of the new groups.

If we didn't have the money for the record we could still hear the latest hit on the radio. Detroit had some great DJ's back then, like Frantic Ernie Durham. He was one of our favorites, because he was always so excited about the latest tunes, and that got us excited, too.

There were other great DJ's as well, like Labaron Taylor and Martha Jean. We'd listen to them in the evening after we did our chores and our homework, and all weekend long.

When we were fifteen, me and Napoleon lied about our age and got jobs as busboys at the Ponchetrain. It was a brand new fancy hotel downtown near the Detroit River. They had live bands, too. I worked there after school, and I used the extra money to buy shoes or hats. I usually had a hat on my head, turned low and looking cool. And, of course, I was always buying the latest 45 single.

Normally, I was a shy kind of young man, especially when I was around girls. We all listened to the latest Motown hits, like *I like it Like That,* by Smokey Robinson and the Miracles, or Little Stevie Wonder's *Fingertips.* We'd get together once a month in the summer and organize a house party. We'd collect twenty-five cents per person to pay for the refreshments.

Shorty's basement was our favorite rendezvous. It was finished, and was the best looking of any of our basements. He had a pool table, and his parents let us have the parties, as long as we kept things in order and didn't get too rowdy. Not only that, but Shorty–his real name is John Morris–was Stevie Wonder's first cousin, and sometimes Stevie would stop by.

We couldn't wait for that Saturday night party. Everyone had to invite ten people. We used to bet on who would get the most girls to come. I was mostly the shy, quiet guy, so I never got more than one or two girls to come to the party. The main guys organizing the parties were me, June and Ball, and Rodney Reno. Usually June and Rodney would get the most girls to come to the party, with Nate and Ball close behind them.

On this weekend we had the latest 45, Little Stevie Wonder's *Fingertips.* We'd gone to Shorty's basement to play it. If my dad was going to be out, they'd come over to my place, and we'd play the new record over and over. We'd know every line, and we'd sing that new song all week long, walking to school or going to work. My mom would cook for all of us, so my house was one of the guys' favorites, the food was always good and plentiful, just like down on the farm. My dad was very strict about girls, and we could never have parties if he was going to be around.

My closest girl at that time was Regina Reno, Rodney Reno's sister. We were so close, we were like brother and sister. We helped each other with our homework. We tried to beat each other at school, seeing who got the better grades, so we were real buddies, and we're still good friends. We never got a romantic relationship going, we just hung out together and talked and went to parties. I brought her and one of her girlfriends to Shorty's basement

Anyway, the guys had put our money together, and we bought a little bottle of courage, which was a wine called Silver Satin. It was so nasty that we had to put Kool Aid in it and hold our nose to drink it, but to us it was worth it, because it gave us the courage we needed to face the girls.

We took turns with the Silver Satin. One bottle didn't go very far, but we were young and not used to drinking, so it didn't take a lot of wine to make us feel relaxed and confident. We were ready to go out and dance with the girls!

The best dancers at the party were Napoleon and June. They would learn the new dances, and then they'd teach us. June and Nate worked hard to get everybody into the dance, so we wouldn't end up holding up the wall and looking dopey. We did the Twist till we were dizzy. After that came the Jerk, which was just like the name says: jerky. After the Jerk came the Mashed-Potato. I could never see how I was supposed to move like a pot of boiled potatoes, but I did my best.

One of the best dances was from a song, *Dancing in the Street*, by Martha and the Vandellas. We moved our feet from side to side, two to the side, then two to the other. It was a good dance, because we all moved together.

At this particular party I had the extra bit of courage in me, and I jumped up on Shorty's pool table and started dancing. My friends Napoleon Ross and Lamont Lawrence were cheering me on.

They hollered, "Go ahead, Delray! You got the moves, boy," and words to that effect. I don't know what got into me. The record player was pumping out a Motown song, I was jumping and spinning on the pool table in Shorty's basement, and everybody was cheering me, then I'd jump off the table, land on the floor, and do a split. I was having the best time of my life.

If we didn't go to Shorty's basement for a party, we would go to dance parties at the Palladium, or the Graystone, or the 20 Grand Ball Room, or the Arcade. We'd see the latest acts and hear the newest songs. At the clubs Nate did most of the dancing, while Lamont and I would watch. Once in a while Nate would drag us onto the dance floor with a girl, but we weren't very good dancers, so we'd run off the dance floor as soon as the music was over.

Of all the Detroit dance parties, the one we loved the most was the Christmas Motown Review. We waited all year for that show, it was the best thing in all of Detroit. It was held downtown at Christmas time. We would save up for our tickets, and we never missed it. We saw the Temptations, the Miracles, Mary Wells, Martha and the Vandellas, Marvin Gaye, and lots of other singers. Those were the very best times for us growing up.

We always wore our best outfit, because it was Christmas time. Since all of us brothers were the same size, we could share our clothes. We all had jobs after school, and most of our money went to buy clothes. I might buy myself a sharkskin suit and a cashmere coat, June might buy a sharp wool suit. We swapped everything: shoes, shirts, shark skin suits and mohair coats. We liked the floppy hats with the wide brims and white cashmere scarves.

Today, the kids wear gym shoes everywhere, but back then, we wore gym shoes for gym. The rest of the time, we wore shoes we polished till they sparkled like diamonds.

One year I thought my dad wouldn't let me go to the Motown Christmas review, I was in so much trouble. I was lucky to even be allowed out of the house on this Saturday. A couple of days before, June, my oldest brother, convinced me to have my hair processed. That meant getting it straightened. I went to the hair salon and had it done. I thought I looked pretty good, but I knew my dad would be mad.

When I got home, I tried to hide my hair under a hat, but my mother saw what I'd done.

She said to my dad, "Albert, do you see what that boy has done to his hair?"

My father pulled off my hat. I knew by the look on his face that I was in trouble.

"Go into the bathroom and wash that out right now!" he told me.

I went into the bathroom and washed my hair, but it just got straighter and straighter.

I came back out. My dad said, "What did I tell you, boy?"

I told him, "I tried, daddy, but the more I wash it, the straighter it gets!"

He told my brother Tony to get the clippers, then he sat me down in the kitchen table and started to cut off all of my hair. I begged him and cried, I didn't want to lose my hair, but it didn't help, he just kept on cutting.

I'd always been proud of my hair. I wore it pretty long, it was the sixties, after all, and I had a good curl in it, too. When he cut off all my hair, it wasn't shaved, so I didn't have that cool bald look, it just looked ugly, like I had a disease that made it fall out. I was ashamed to be seen in public.

I put on a hat to hide my ugly head and went to the Motown Christmas Review with Nate and Preacher and June, Rodney Reno, Lamont, Ball and Tony. No matter how ugly I looked, nothing was keeping me from that party. My dad even felt a little sorry for me, seeing my head all shaved, and he let me go.

We caught the bus on Dexter and took it over to Woodward, then we rode the Woodward bus downtown. There were a lot of cars with big engines rumbling down Woodward Ave. It was the time of muscle cars. Guys drove down Woodward, the Main Street of the Motor City, in big Pontiac GTO's, Barracudas, Bonnevilles and Caddies. They would put straight-through exhaust pipes on the cars, which made the engines rumble so loud they shook the ground. Music poured from their open windows, even in the freezing temperatures, and big cars ruled the streets.

The bunch of us tumbled off the bus in front of the Motown Fox Theatre, on Woodward downtown. There was snow on the ground. Once it snowed in Detroit, it stuck for most of the winter, it was that cold.

There were lots of people standing waiting to go inside. Everybody was dressed up in their best, nice long cuts. The girls all looked great, dressed in their new Christmas outfits. They wore boots with high heels, short leather coats, leather gloves and hats. And jewelry sparkling in the neon lights like smiles and laughter.

The guys wore cashmere coats with colored scarves that went

with the coats. They all had hats, too: felt hats, leather hats, corduroy hats, anything to sit on a head full of curly hair. They all wore good suits, with shirts and ties, and polished shoes

The theatre was lit up so bright it was as light as day in front. It was a mostly black audience, two thousand African-Americans, with a sprinkling of whites. Most were young, but there were a lot of older folks, too.

There were three lines to buy tickets. We entered the theatre and walked through a big hallway. You could go upstairs to the balcony, but we preferred to go down to the orchestra section. There were no reserved seats, it was strictly first come first served. We got there early, so we found seats in the middle, where you had the best view and the sound was great.

The MC was Frantic Ernie Durham. He was a disc jockey for WJLB, a Detroit radio station that played a lot of Motown and R&B. Ernie was light-skinned, thin, frail-looking. He wasn't a real big guy, just average height. The thing that he had that made him great was his unique voice. He had a real radio voice. It resonated. He was the king of the DJs. When he rolled his name, Ff-rantic Er-nie Dur-ham, the whole crowd got excited. He could really raise his voice and roll his RRR's. It was a voice that grabbed you and picked you up with every announcement.

We saw The Temptations. The lead singer, David Ruffin, belted out the song, with Eddie Kendriks and Paul Williams all taking turns with the lead. Their faces glowed in the lights. They sang *My Girl*, their biggest hit, *Beauty is Only Skin Deep, Ain't Too Proud To Beg*, and other great tunes. When Melvin Franklin, the bass singer, hit those low notes the whole crowd stood up and cheered. We loved the way he sang.

The Supremes, with Diana Ross leading, came on and sang *Stop in the Name of Love*, the back-up singers twisting and smiling and pouring out the feeling. They did *Baby Love*, a sweet, sexy song. *Come See About Me* was their top hit that year, and the audience was standing and dancing with the music by then. We couldn't get enough of the Supremes, they were so good.

Smokey Robinson and the Miracles came on next. Smokey sang *Tracks of My Tears*, which got the audience seated and quiet. Then he belted out a really hot song, *Shop Around*, and we were up on our feet again, dancing and clapping.

Martha and the Vandellas came on stage. Martha sang *No-*

where to Run, Nowhere to Hide. We loved her singing. She followed that with *Heat Wave*, and we liked that song even more. There were so many great acts, like the Marvelettes. Marvin Gaye sang *I'll be Doggone*, and *Try It, Baby*. We felt like we were in Heaven and the heavenly choirs were pouring out the music.

After the show we went to the White Castle on Woodward and hung out. We ordered a cheeseburger or a fish sandwich, coffee or coke, and we talked about the show, going over the songs, talking about which was the best. It was impossible to choose the best, there were so many great acts.

When our last nickel was gone we rode the bus back home up Woodward Avenue. As we split up, we knew that our Christmas was complete. We didn't need Santa Claus. Didn't care about any reindeer. We had heard the best music in the world. Those songs would be on our lips and in our ears, carrying us all together through the holidays and into the New Year. The music lifted us up and buoyed our spirits. It made us happy, and in the sharing of it, the music brought us together.

CHAPTER FIFTEEN

When I was fifteen my brothers thought I would never get a girlfriend, I was so shy. I had my friend, Regina, Rodney Reno's sister, but she was just like a sister to me, everyone knew that.

One day, my brother Tony came to me. He said, "Delray, this girl around the corner likes you. She wants you to come around to her aunt's house." He said her name was Yvonne. She didn't go to my high school, but she'd seen me around the neighborhood playing ball and such.

I was reading my sports paper. I just told him, "Get out of here, Slow, I don't want to meet no girl."

I just kept reading my paper, but secretly I did want to meet her.

He said, "You're not scared of a little girl, are you?"

I told him, "Of course I'm not scared of no girl. I just don't want to meet her, is all."

But Slow kept bugging me and bugging me. He even offered to introduce me

"I'll do all the talking," he promised. "You just got to meet her. Okay?"

"I don't have to open my mouth?" I asked. I didn't think I would be able to talk to her without a little bit of Silver Satin courage.

"That's right," he said. "You let me do the talking."

Finally, after he bugged me for about a week, I agreed.

I walked over to her aunt's house with Tony. When we got to her house, I stood on the sidewalk and I told Tony, "You go to the door."

"Okay," he said, "but don't run out on me."

He went up and knocked on the door. Yvonne came out with one of her cousins. It looked like they were expecting us. She told me her name was Yvonne, and, of course, she knew my name already. We went to a restaurant in the neighborhood called Big Daddy's, where we sat and talked. Tony went off with the cousin, and I stayed and kept on talking with Yvonne.

She was a petite girl, just a tickle over five feet tall. She had a dark complexion and a nice figure. She was a warm, friendly, caring person. I liked her right away. It wasn't long before I felt comfortable with her, and the more we talked, the more I got over my shyness.

When it was time for us to go home she gave me her telephone number and I gave her mine. I told Yvonne, "If my father answers, pretend you have the wrong number. He's very strict. He doesn't want me going out with a girl; he thinks I'm too young."

Pretty soon, Yvonne and I were going steady. We talked on the phone every day. She went to a different high school than me; she went to Western, I went to Northwestern, so we didn't get to walk to school together.

At first we only saw each other on the weekends. We'd go to the movies. After the show, we'd go somewhere, usually Big Daddy's, Mama's, or Peppy's, and get something to eat.

One evening, after we'd been seeing each other for a few months, Yvonne reached around my neck and unclasped the gold chain I was wearing. She put it around hers, and she smiled in this knowing, satisfied way. She said that the chain was a bond that held us together.

We had a tradition back then where the girl would take something of sentimental value of yours and keep it for herself. It was a symbol that you were going steady.

We dated for two years. Then one day Yvonne found out she was pregnant. We decided right away that we would get married. I was seventeen; she was sixteen. Neither one of us had any doubts about it, because we knew we were right for each other.

I still had dreams of playing baseball for the Tigers, but when I decided to marry Yvonne, I put my dreams aside, at least for the immediate future. My first priority was to raise my family. I wanted to give them a better life than I had growing up. My dad and mom grew up poor in little farms down south without running water. They moved up north to Detroit to give us kids a better life, which we had. Even though I grew up poor, my brothers and sisters and I were much better off then my parents were when they were kids. Now I was determined to see that my children did even better.

It was the sixties, the time of Martin Luther King, Jr., and Malcolm X. There was a lot of talk about change. Talk of civil rights, and opportunities for blacks. I wanted those opportunities for my children, and I thanked God they were growing up in a period when jobs were opening up for them.

That was what life was all about: seeing that your children had a better life than you did.

I was working at the Warren Truck Plant, on the midnight to 8 shift. After I graduated from high school in June, 1967, I took a second job at Chevy Gear and Axle. Yvonne got a job at a local hamburger shop called Peppy's.

We married on October 28, 1967. I was just two months shy of eighteen. Yvonne was sixteen, and still in high school. The day of the wedding, Nate and Pug tried to get me drunk. They hoped that I would miss my wedding. They were afraid that when I got married we wouldn't be able to go out and have fun together the way we always did.

I told them that my being married might slow me down a little, especially with the baby coming, but we would still have time together. Most of my friends weren't ready to accept adult responsibilities. They wanted to be single and free, but I was ready to be a family man, even though I was only coming up to eighteen.

The wedding was a small event. It was at her mother and father's home. My pastor married us, Rev. William Wilson, of the Oakland Baptist Church, which was the church I attended.

We had a reception; about 75 people came to it. Yvonne wore a pink dress, I wore a black suit. We were a happy young couple hoping for a good future for our family. We had a good chance of making it, there was plenty of work for me at the auto plant. We were young and happy, with our first child on the way. The future was bright with promise.

We stayed with my folks most of the time. Sometimes we stayed at her parent's house. We lived like that while we saved for an apartment and furniture. With me working two jobs and Yvonne working at Peppy's, it didn't take too long before we moved into a place on Lindwood.

Early one morning, a few months after we were married, Yvonne woke me.

"The bed's wet," she told me.

At first I didn't understand what she meant. Then I realized that her bag of waters had broken. She was having contraction pains. I called my dad. He came right over in the car. Yvonne and I piled into the back seat, and off we went to Hutzel Hospital. Yvonne was crying, and my dad was telling her she was going to be fine. He'd been through it so many times, he was very relaxed and calming.

Me, I was scared and happy and excited all at the same time, and I was glad I had my dad with me, because nothing ever rattled him or got him scared. He could handle anything.

Our daughter Monique was born, on December 16, 1967. We brought her home, and for the first time, I knew what it was like to have somebody who was mine. Really, truly mine. Of course, Monique was as much Yvonne's child as she was mine. But having a child was different than having brothers and sisters and parents. For the first time I had somebody in my life who was *my* responsibility. Monique was my pride, my joy, my reason to go to work, my future. She was everything to me.

She was my daughter.

Kim was born a year later, on November 25, 1968. I had the same feeling for her that I had for Monique. She was an easy baby to hold and take care of. She slept and ate and gurgled and cooed. I would scoop her up in my arms, wanting to protect her from every harm and every pain.

We dressed them alike, they were only eleven months apart. We "twinned them", as my dad said, and most people took them as twins.

Yvonne and I were very happy together. I couldn't ask for a better wife. She kept the apartment nice and clean, she was a loving mother, and she was always there by my side. We got along fine. I wasn't as good about saving as she was, so Yvonne always held some money back. We never got in trouble with the bills.

We shared our dreams–beautiful hopes for the future. We wanted to move out of Detroit into a better neighborhood. Our children would have a good school and go to college. Yvonne would go to college, too. She wanted to study business administration. And I still dreamed of playing for the Tigers, just like my hero, Willie Horton, who graduated from my high school.

But now, lying in my hospital bed, all covered with bandages and feeling the pain, I had more fears than I had hopes. I waited every day for my wife to visit me. She came in as often as she could, and she tried to be brave, but she still had that same look of panic on her face she had that first day in the hospital. As the weeks wore on, the look of fear never left her face. I could still see it in her eyes, hear it in her voice.

She tried to be supportive and say the right things, but she just wasn't tough, like my dad was, or like Ball. She was more like my mom, vulnerable and anxious. Her eyes gave away what she was truly feeling. She was scared to look at me, and that look on her face just about broke my heart.

I tried to keep a brave face, too, for her sake. I asked her how the girls were. Yvonne said the girls were fine. She couldn't bring them to the hospital, of course, there were restrictions on the age of the visitors. But even if the hospital allowed it, it would only frighten them to see me, so I didn't even think about asking Yvonne to bring them to the hospital.

As the weeks turned into months, Yvonne began to visit me less and less often. I got more and more scared that I was losing her. Not just losing her, my wife, but my children, as well. I was afraid that if she left me she would take the kids with her. Maybe even move to another town. Or another state.

I had always been the kind of guy who would help a friend if they needed something. My mom and dad were that way, and I took after them. Now it looked like I might be losing the three people that I cherished the most. It seemed so completely unfair; as unjust as the fire that nearly killed me.

I asked myself, is this the reward I get for trying to lead my life in a good way?

My mom tried to keep me in contact with my daughters by visiting Yvonne and the girls often. She would tell me what the girls were doing, what they were wearing, what Monique, the older one, was saying and all. She always brought me good news. My mother was careful to only tell me that things were going well for them. She didn't want me to worry about my family, I had enough to worry about surviving day to day.

Marlene, my favorite nurse, told my father to bring pictures of the kids, and he did. Marlene put them on the table by my bed, so I could see them whenever I woke up.

I knew that I wasn't going to be much help to her until I recovered, and that might be for a long while. I wanted her to wait for me, but I was afraid that it would take so long for me to get back on my feet, she wouldn't be able to hold out that long. She was only sixteen when we married. We loved each other, and we got along real good before the fire, but I didn't really know if she was the kind of girl who could stand by me while I was so terribly sick.

It wasn't anything against my wife. Some people can handle a tragedy, even a terrible one like mine. They accept their fate, roll up their sleeves, and make the best of it. That was how my mother was. She would have stood by my father if he were ever injured or sick. If he had a stroke and was paralyzed and lived the rest of his life in a wheelchair, just sitting and looking out the front window, she would take care of him every day. But not everyone can give up the things they want and dream about out of love or duty. I was afraid Yvonne might be like that.

In the beginning, it was hard for me to see *her* side of things. But with all that time I had to think, eventually I began to see that life wasn't just hard for me, it was hard for Yvonne, too. She was young and pretty. She didn't know what do to with her life, if she should stick with me, or find somebody else who was healthy and could provide for her and her daughter.

I was scared that she would take up with another man. That thought drove me crazy. But at the same time I couldn't blame her for not sticking it out the way my brothers and sisters and parents and Napoleon and Lamont were doing. They had all been with me my whole life; she only knew me for two years.

Maybe I was being selfish, but I needed her.

One day, I noticed the baby who used to cry at night was gone. I asked Marlene if she was transferred out to the floor. She told me, yes, the baby was doing better and was out on the pediatric wing. I asked if I could visit her, but Marlene said I couldn't, I was too sick to leave the Intensive Care Unit. Maybe I could visit when I got stronger, she said.

I was happy for the baby and for her mother. I imagined that she would grow up strong and healthy, and she would forget her burns. But my future didn't look bright at all. Mine looked just the opposite: dark and hopeless.

I didn't believe that I would be healed and grow to be healthy the way that the baby would. Even if I did make it out of the Intensive Care Unit alive, it looked like I was losing my family.

This was the lowest time in my life. What was the point of living if I had to go on without my wife and daughters? Family was everything. It was the reason to live, the reason to go to work, the reason to sacrifice. The family gave me a purpose.

There was a coldness creeping into Yvonne's voice that sent shivers down my spine. It was the same kind of feeling I had when I watched the clock on the wall in the Intensive Care Unit and knew that the time for my dressing change was surely coming.

CHAPTER SIXTEEN

In May, 1969, four months after Delbert McCoy was taken to Detroit General, Eugene Kelley went on trial before Judge Frank G. Shemanske for setting the fire at the Soul Expression Club. Kelley's Chicago friend, Ronald Robinson, the second suspect, was still at large, and so he did not testify at Kelley's trial.

Back in April, Theodore Wallace, the Detroit man who drove the getaway car, made a deal with the District Attorney. The D.A. only charged him with malicious destruction of property, a misdemeanor crime, and not the more serious crime or arson, or attempted murder. Wallace pled guilty to the charge. In exchange for the lesser charges, he promised to testify against the main suspects. Wallace was sentenced to ninety days in jail, and was still incarcerated when Kelley came to trial.

According to Wallace's testimony, on the night of the fire Robinson borrowed Kelley's coat and left it at the Soul Expression. He went back to the club to get the coat. When the bouncer Alvin Gunn wouldn't let Robinson back in without paying another dollar, Robinson vowed to "burn the place down" if they didn't let him in.

Robinson told Wallace to take him to a gas station. Wallace drove to a Marathon station a few blocks from the Soul Expression. At the station, Robinson and Kelley bought a two gallon can of gas.

There were two friends of Wallace in the car, Ulysses Butts and Donald Jones. At the time of the arrests, a judge let Butts and Jones go free, with all charges against them dropped. They testified against Kelley and Robinson, along with Theodore Wallace, the driver.

The testimony of Butts and Jones supported Wallace's account that Kelley and Robinson bought the can of gas from the Marathon Station a few blocks away from the club. The gas station attendant testified to the same. He told the jury how Robinson didn't have enough money to leave a deposit for the two-gallon can, so Robinson took off his black onyx ring and left it as collateral.

The District Attorney then brought out the ring, with the black stone. The attendant identified it as Robinson's. It was devastating evidence. The ring made it personal. It showed that Robinson was determined to set the fire.

Wallace further testified that he drove back to the Soul Expression, where Robinson got out of the car. Robinson beckoned to

Kelley, saying "Come on." The two of them walked into the club together, with Robinson carrying the can of gasoline. A moment later,
the two came running out, and flames flew out from the doorway. It
was a very fast fire. Even before they could get down the street, smoke
and fire were shooting out from the building.

    Wallace also testified that, when Kelley and Robinson ran back
into the car, Robinson said, "You [Kelley] threw the match too quick."
Wallace went on to say that Kelley didn't deny throwing the match at
all. Kelley kept quiet, without protesting his innocence.

    The D.A. got Wallace to admit that, as he drove his car away
from the club, he could hear the cries of the teenagers trapped inside.
The courtroom was hushed; even judge Shemanske looked stunned at
such callous behavior.

    Robinson's words, as recounted by Wallace and his friends,
hung his friend Kelley, even though Kelley's defense lawyer never got
to confront Robinson.

    When it was his turn to testify, Kelley got on the stand and
denied everything. He claimed he was an innocent bystander. He said
that Robinson had done it all. Robinson bought the gasoline, Robinson
carried the can into the vestibule, and Robinson poured it onto the
floor. Kelley even claimed that Robinson asked him for a match.

    Kelley testified that he told Robinson, "I don't have any
matches, I don't smoke." The way Kelley told it, Robinson reached
into Kelley's coat, which he had borrowed earlier in the evening, pulled
out a book of matches, struck a match, and tossed it on the fire.

    But the jury didn't buy Kelley's story. Too many people heard
it happen differently. Besides, the D.A. argued, if Kelley didn't smoke,
why was he carrying matches in his coat pocket? But the most damn-
ing evidence against Kelley came from another eyewitness: a victim
of the firebombing–Delbert McCoy.

Dr. Grifka told me it was time for me to give my testimony. I
had to testify in the hospital, because I was much too sick to go to the
courtroom. I only weighed sixty pounds, so Dr. Grifka and Moses,
the orderly, were able to pick me up and gently lowered me down into
the wheelchair. It was painful, but I could handle it.

    Moses wheeled me down to a conference room. Marlene was
right there beside me, too. There were a lot of people in the room. My
dad was there waiting, like he always was. There was a judge sitting at

a table, Judge Shemanske. There was a bunch of people seated together; the District Attorney explained that they were the jury. I was glad that they got a chance to see me, it meant that they would get a real good sense of how much damage the arsonists had caused.

I understood that a lot of people were hurt in the fire at the Soul Expression. I wasn't the only one that was injured. It would have been selfish of me to think that my troubles were all there was to the charges against the fire bombers.

They swore me in, and then the District Attorney asked me to tell him what happened on the night of the fire. I told them that there were two men standing outside the Soul Expression talking. One of them told me, "You better not go in there, were' fixin' to do something." He looked angry or upset, I wasn't sure which.

A couple of minutes later, I saw two men come into the vestibule. One of them poured the gasoline, the other one threw the match. I remembered that quite clearly.

The judge them asked me, did I identify a person in photos that the police showed me? I said, "Yes, sir, I did."

The Judge asked me how many pictures were there. He wanted to know did any of the detectives coach me to select one person out of the pictures, or did I just happen to pick a photo that I recognized?

I told him nobody coached me. The photos were just put in front of me one at a time. As soon as I saw Kelly, I told the detectives, that was the guy.

The judge asked me, how could I be sure he was the same man. I told him that I couldn't forget the face, because just before I entered the Soul Expression, Kelly looked right at me and told me, "Man, I wouldn't go up there, something's going to happen."

It made me hesitate, the way he talked and looked, but I didn't think much about it at the time.

Then the District Attorney asked if I could identify Kelley right there in the conference room. I told him I couldn't do it, my eyes had gone bad. Because of the damage to my eyelids and face, I couldn't blink or close my eyes properly. That caused me to sleep with my eyes partly open. They dried out and got infected, and that made my vision blurry.

My eyes were okay the first couple of weeks I was in the hospital. That was why I was able to pick out Kelley from the photographs the detectives showed me. But by the time the trial came around, I could only testify to what I saw on the day of the fire, not whether the defendant on trial was the guy I saw that night.

Kelley's defense attorney wanted to throw out my testimony, on account of my not being able to identify Kelley right then and there, but the Judge overruled him. The Judge said that my identifying Kelley in the photo was "admissible." As a result, my testimony still carried a lot of weight.

The District Attorney explained to the jury that it was significant how I remembered there were *two* men acting *together*, not one acting while the other was just standing by watching. My testimony proved that one man poured the gasoline, the other one threw the match. That meant that it didn't matter which role Kelley played, he still shared responsibility for the fire with his friend, Robinson.

The judge accepted my testimony. He thanked me for leaving my hospital bed and coming to testify, and then he let me go back to my room. He was very patient and understanding, like Dr. Grifka. Marlene and the orderly wheeled me back to my room.

The most important testimony given at trial was Wallace's statement that he heard Robinson saying to Kelley, "You threw the match too quick!" Kelley's lawyer objected. He said that Kelley had the right to challenge his accuser, Robinson. Unfortunately for Kelley, Robinson was still at large, and so could not be called before the court as a witness. But Wallace, Butts and Jones, who were in the car that night, had all repeated the same story.

Kelley's defense lawyer tried vigorously to have the testimony of Kelley, Butts and Jones thrown out as hearsay. The judge allowed the testimony because it was uttered in an emotional state, and so, under the law, it was unlikely to be a fabrication.

The Judge pointed out that, even if they did find Robinson and bring him to court, there was no way to compel him to testify, because Robinson had the right to remain silent if his words could lead to his own conviction. So Robinson's absence was a moot point.

The Judge told the jury to consider Eugene Kelley's guilt or innocence on three counts of arson. The counts were, (1) willfully or maliciously burning real property; (2), placing, using or distributing any inflammable, combustible or explosive material in or about any building with intent to willfully and maliciously burn; and (3), placing explosives with intent to destroy property with resulting personal injury.

Once again, Kelley's lawyer objected. He said that gasoline was not an explosive device, and so the third count should be thrown out. Then he went on to argue that, if the third count was thrown out, the other two should be discarded as well.

Judge Shemanske wasn't buying any of it. He told the defense lawyer that it was common knowledge that gasoline was an explosive. Every time you started your car, the gasoline in the cylinder exploded hundreds of time, each explosion driving the piston hard enough to accelerate a three-thousand pound vehicle. Gasoline, he said, was a very impressive explosive.

The Judge let the jury consider all three counts of the indictment. They didn't waste any time. In just a little over an hour they came out and found Kelley guilty on all three counts.

Judge Shemanske thanked the jurors and dismissed them. Then, he made Kelley stand up to hear his sentence. The judge gave Kelley 2 1/2-10 years for the first two counts, which was what the law required. For the third count, use of an explosive device to do harm, he gave Kelley the maximum sentence—life in prison without chance for parole.

My dad and my Uncle Treetop were at the trial. After the jury found Kelley guilty and the judge announced the sentence, and after Kelley was led away, my dad went up to the judge to thank him for what he ruled. The judge told my dad that he wanted to give Kelly the death penalty, but the law wouldn't allow him to do it, so he did the next best thing. He gave Kelly a sentence of life without parole.

"It was the best I could do," the judge said.

My dad thanked him again. Then he left the courtroom and came to the hospital to tell me what happened.

CHAPTER SEVENTEEN

When my weight got down to fifty-seven pounds, my dad said I looked like a prisoner of war. Dr. Grifka told him that if I didn't get more weight on me, I wasn't going to make it. The hospital was feeding me pureed food, because I still couldn't open my mouth very far. That food was like baby food, only it had even less flavor. It was horrible. I could barely get it down.

My mom asked Dr. Grifka if she could cook and bring food in for me. He said that would be okay, so long as it was very soft and I didn't have to chew it much. Mom and my sisters, Gwen and Jackie, started to bring in homemade food. They ground it up until it was soft and I didn't hardly have to chew it at all, but still it tasted great. It was so much better than the hospital food. I started putting on weight right away.

My mom always cooked lots of food for us when we were young. Even if we didn't have much money, she made sure there was always food on the table. Every Fall she put up vegetables from our garden in jars, so we had them all winter long. I guess it came from her growing up on a farm, where you might not have a dollar, but you always had something to eat.

All the kids in the neighborhood were welcome in her kitchen. When we came in after school for a snack, we usually had our friends with us. Nate, Pug (Lamont Lawrence), Preacher (Alan Lawrence), Shorty, who let us hang out in his finished basement, and lots more. My mom would spread out hot biscuits and butter and jam, hot chocolate in the winter, lemonade in the spring and summer. We didn't *feel* poor, even though we didn't have much money, because we were rich in friendships and family.

When I think of my childhood I always remember waking up in the morning and hearing my mom downstairs getting out the pots and pans and cooking. I remember the sound of bacon sizzling on the grill, and the smells from the oven when she took out the biscuits and the corn bread, and the odor of strong coffee she served for my dad.

The smells would come up the stairs and tickle my nose, and I'd be wide awake. There was no use trying to go back to sleep, the promise of breakfast was too strong to stay in bed. Coming downstairs, I would see my mother in her long pioneer apron, rolling out the dough and making everything from scratch. If it was a weekend, chances are Jackie or Gwen or both of them would be helping.

As I lay in my hospital bed, I wished that I could be back in her kitchen watching her cook and smelling all the good smells. Even though I knew it would be a while before I was back there, I still had the memories, strong and clear, and they kept me going through the days and nights in the hospital. And now, after having to eat the horrible hospital pureed food, I had my mom's good home cooking to sustain me, even if she had to heat it up in the hospital's little pantry.

As my weight started coming back I felt a little stronger. I was getting new skin grafts every week or two, and I was getting out of bed into the chair, even though it was still painful to be moved. I still needed a blood transfusion nearly every day, but the water in the tank didn't turn as bright red as it used to, so I figured I was doing a little better.

After six months in the Intensive Care Unit, Dr. Grifka told me I was ready to go out to the medical floor. I wanted to go, it meant I was one step closer to going home. But at the same time I was scared of losing Marlene and the other nurses and orderlies who had watched over me. In the ICU someone is always close by to hear your voice. I knew that on the floor nobody could see you unless they came into your room. You could go without seeing a nurse or an aide for a long time. That was a very scary thought.

I finally told Dr. Grifka that I would go out of the ICU, but before I left, there was one thing that I had to do. I had to look at my face. I hadn't looked in a mirror since the day of the fire. I'd seen my arms and legs when the doctors removed my bandages, but not my face.

Everybody who treated me in the Intensive Care Unit was always very compassionate. They never looked at me funny or made a comment to each other when they took off my bandages and saw the extent of my injuries. Even so, I worried about how bad I looked. Out on the medical floor, a lot more people would see me. When the dressings were removed and strangers saw my face, I was scared about how they would react.

Heck, I was worried about how *I* would react. I got Marlene to bring me a mirror. After she unwrapped the bandages from my face, I told her to hold the mirror up for me to see, I couldn't hold it myself, my fingers were bandaged together.

Seeing my face in the mirror was a terrible shock. Before the burn I never thought that I was a particularly good-looking guy, but the face that stared back at me in the mirror was horrible. It had scars and patches of raw, bloody skin. The eyes didn't have any lashes or eyebrows, the skull didn't have any hair, and the mouth was swollen and pink. It didn't even look like me.

But the worst part was the ears. *They were gone!* Both of my ears were burned away. I had flat skin and two holes on the sides of my head, but no ear lobes.

It was bad, and I cried like a baby. Marlene tried to comfort me, but it was no use. I was very down. I didn't see any hope at all. I began to understand why my mom found it so hard to stay with me; and I realized that Yvonne had even more trouble looking at me. I wasn't the young man she married less than two years ago.

I prayed to God to give me strength to go on living, but I was in the deepest graveyard of despair. I didn't believe that God would be able to lift me out of my depression. How could I face the world when my face was disfigured and ugly? How could my children look at me or kiss me good-night? How could my pretty young wife ever love me when I looked the way I did?

It seemed like there was no hope . . .no hope at all for me. What was the use of me surviving the fire and getting all of the skin grafts and blood transfusions and operations when the person that was saved was so hideous?

Marlene tried hard to be reassuring. She was very sweet and kind. She told me there was a lot of plastic surgery they could do. She said I shouldn't get too down by how I looked right now, it was way too soon to give up. Marlene was very sincere and optimistic. I wanted to believe her, but the face that looked back on me in the mirror was so torn up, I didn't think that I could ever go out and meet people again. And I didn't believe that the doctors would ever be able to make me look close to normal.

Dr. Grifka also tried to comfort me. He told me that my face would not always be so red and swollen; the swelling would go down. He said there would be plenty of time for reconstructive surgery, but that kind of plastic surgery had to wait until all of my wounds were healed up. He was very encouraging, and he left me with a little bit of hope; a flicker of light in the darkness.

The doctor told me that when I left the Intensive Care Unit he was going to put me in a special bed called a Circle Electric Bed. The bed was going to turn me upside down without my having to roll over. That would let me get off my back and protect me from bedsores.

I had enough sores on my body without getting new ones from lying in bed all the time, so that sounded pretty good to me. But when the orderly, Moses Young, wheeled me out of the Intensive Care and into my new room, I got my first look at the Circle Electric Bed. It scared the hell out of me. It looked like a ride for an amusement park in Hell.

I told Dr. Grifka, "I don't want to get in it."

He said, "You have to get in the bed, Delbert."

"How long do I have to stay in that thing?" I asked.

"It shouldn't be more than two or three months," said Dr. Grifka. " It's better than turning you in the regular bed."

It was true, turning me in the bed was very painful. I couldn't stand people to grab my body and roll me, or to reposition my arms and legs, which you have to do if you're going to roll onto your side. Something as simple as shifting my hips was still extremely painful. Turning was unbearable.

I looked at the bed some more. It was made up of two big steel frames forming circles, about six feet across. The two circles were attached to a base with a motor that turned the frame.

"What if the whole thing falls over? It don't look too stable."

Dr. Grifka told me the bed was perfectly safe. And besides, it would get my burns to heal quicker.

I didn't like the look of that Circle Electric, but I trusted Dr. Grifka. He had been straight with me from day one. I didn't want to disappoint him, so I let Marlene and Moses lift me off the stretcher and put me in the Circle Electric Bed on my back.

It wasn't much of a bed. The mattress wasn't nearly as soft as the bed in the Intensive Care Unit. It was very narrow, only a little more than half as wide as a regular bed, and it was lumpy and hard.

Nurse Pfeifer, the nurse who would be taking care of me on the ward, put straps across my hips and chest and tightened them. That made me nervous. They had never strapped me down before.

"It's because the bed is narrow and doesn't have any side rails," the new nurse explained.

"Why don't you show him how the bed works?" said Marlene. "It'll make him feel better."

The new nurse placed a leather strap across my face. It covered my forehead and my chin. She tightened the leather, and that hurt, but it wasn't too bad. I felt a little like an astronaut.

Next, the nurse picked up a duplicate of the narrow mattress that I was laying on. I could see that it had a metal frame on one side, which explained why it was so lumpy. She put the second mattress right on top of me, so that the front of my body was pressed against it. Then she tightened some screws at the head and foot that held the two mattresses together.

I was just like a hunk of meat wrapped up tight in a deli sandwich.

The nurse picked up a control panel and pressed a button. The electric motor hummed and the bed started to rotate. All of a sudden I found my head starting to go up and my legs going down. After a minute, I was straight up and down. I got scared, thinking I was gong to slide right out of the bed onto the floor, but Marlene and Nurse Pfeifer reassured me that I wouldn't slip out.

Nurse Pfeifer kept pressing the button, and now my head was going down. Pretty soon, I was lying on my stomach, looking straight down at the floor. She stopped the bed from rotating just as I got level again, otherwise, I would have ended up standing on my head.

She unstrapped the mattress I used to be lying on and pulled it off my back. Then, she covered me with a sheet, and there I was, turned like an egg over easy, staring down at the linoleum.

It wasn't just the bed that was different from the ICU. The room was also very isolated. Although Dr. Grifka had warned me and my family that they had a lot less staff on the wards than they did in the Intensive Care Unit, it was still a shock when I found myself alone for long periods of time.

My loneliness was worse because at first I didn't have a roommate. I was glad in a way, I didn't want anybody to have to look at me all day long. But at the same time there was nobody around when I needed help with something. That made it rough.

In the Intensive Care Unit there were always people near my bed or walking by. That made it easy for me to tell them what I needed, I just had to speak to them. But on the ward a patient has to be able to call for the nurse by pushing a button, called a call bell. That was something that I couldn't do, on account of my hands were wrapped in a fist and wouldn't even open. I didn't have any use of my finger, so I wasn't able to push a button.

I was scared that something would happen to me or I would

need something and I wouldn't be to tell anyone. Nurse Pfeifer assured me that somebody would look on me often and that I would be okay. Still, I had my doubts.

When they first started changing my dressings in the Intensive Care Unit, Dr. Grifka tried to straighten my fingers so they wouldn't get contracted and lock up. But the pain was too terrible to bear. It was beyond human endurance, even with the morphine. After the first few days, they gave up trying to open my hands and separate the fingers.

By the time I got to the ward, both my hands were frozen into fists that wouldn't open. The fingers were fused together, too. They were beginning to heal together, like they were webbed. Even bending my arm and reaching out was next to impossible. Pushing the call button to call the nurse was out of the question.

At first I had to call out or just wait for somebody to come in my room in order to make my needs known to anybody. Calling out, "Nurse! Nurse!" got some of the staff angry. They didn't like to hear a patient yelling. It upset the other patients. It probably made it look a little like they were ignoring someone, too.

In the first month or so I had the feeling that the nurses sometimes made me wait before they came into my room, on account of my yelling. It was like they were punishing me for calling out. Like they resented me. Maybe they didn't understand how helpless I was. I couldn't even turn the page of the newspaper to read the sports. I had to wait for someone to come into the room.

I would lie on my stomach with the newspaper spread on the floor underneath me. I'd read the two pages that were open, then I would have to wait for somebody to come in and turn the page. It was very frustrating, not just for me, but for the staff, too. They were a lot busier than the nurses in the ICU, and they probably had better things to do than to turn the page for some guy stuck in a room.

Another problem between the nurses and me was my pain medication. They were worried that I was going to end up a drug addict, and it seemed like they took a long time to get me the medication. I was in a lot of pain, but they acted like I was an addict who shouldn't be given his fix. I had the idea that they almost didn't believe that the burns all over my body caused me terrible pain. I had a lot of trouble in the beginning getting my pain medicine when I thought it was due, until they realized that my pain was real and I had to have my medicine.

They gave me the medicine in my muscle, except most of my

muscles were burned up. My skin was thick and dry, and it was painful getting the needle. But they weren't allowed to give me the morphine directly into my blood stream through the intravenous line. That was something they only did in the Intensive Care Unit. Before long I was full of hard, sore areas where the needle had irritated me.

But after a couple of weeks we got used to each other. The nurses found out that I wasn't really a complaining kind of person. If I hollered, I really needed something. At the same time I got used to the fact that they couldn't come down whenever I called, because they had so many other patients to care for. They didn't have the time to spend with me like they did on the Intensive Care Unit. In the ICU a nurse took care of only one or two patients, but on the floor the nurse had to look after eight or ten patients. Even more on the weekend and at night.

Once we got to understanding each other we got along great. I became part of their routine. Turn Delbert in the bed, turn on the radio, get a game on the station, and open the newspaper. As long as I had my routine, I was okay.

There were two orderlies who worked there, Moses Young and Mr. Johnson. Both of them looked to me like they were retired military, like my dad. Moses was short and solid. He was built like a train. When it was time to get me out of bed, I tried to beg out of it, telling Moses I didn't feel good and I was in a lot of pain, but he wouldn't accept my excuses.

Moses got me out and in the chair, or onto a stretcher and down to the tank for my treatment and dressing change. He was strict, like my dad and my grandfather on the farm. If something had to get done, you did it, and there was no getting out of a chore.

Mr. Johnson, the other orderly, was a little older, but he wasn't any softer. He joked around a lot to cheer me up, but when it was time for the dressing change, he didn't stand for any delay, either. It was up on the stretcher and down to the tank, and no turning back. It was like, "Full speed ahead", right into battle.

My wounds were slowly healing; that was encouraging. And my dad didn't have to sit up with me all night, like he did when I was in the ICU. That made me feel better for his sake. But I was still worried about my wife and my kids. I couldn't help it; I was scared that I would never be a real father for them. If I couldn't be a father, would they be part of my life? I didn't want another man raising my kids, so of course I worried a lot about that. I wanted to hug them so much, but I had no strength in my arms. It was hard to see how I could provide for them the way that I did before the fire.

My mom and dad would bring me messages from the kids. They brought drawings the girls made and pictures of them in new outfits and such. Gwen and my mom visited them a lot, so I always had news about my daughters. That made me feel a little better.

But still I worried. How could I get back home to my family? What work could I get so that I could provide for them? What sort of father would my daughters know: would it be a man they were afraid of, or a man they loved?

The future was full of questions that nobody could answer.

CHAPTER EIGHTEEN

When I was on the ward, the days were filled with long, lonely hours. There were two things that made the time go by and lighten my spirits – visits from family and friends, and sports. The best part of the day was the visit from my family and friends. Somebody came to see me almost every day. I looked forward to their visits so much, I'm sure I wouldn't have been able to keep my hope alive without them.

Following sports teams was the second thing that kept my spirits up. I focused on what the sports teams were doing. I read the sports section of the Daily News over and over, and I listened to any game that was on the radio.

My mom and my sisters visited me a lot more often once I was out on the ward. Their visits always cheered me up. In the beginning I had the room to myself, and they could hang out with me as long as they wanted without getting in the way. Not only that, but they could bring Monique and Kim in for me to see, there not being restrictions on children like they had in the ICU.

I didn't get to see my daughters while I was in the Intensive Care Unit, and I was anxious to have them with me. At the same time, I was nervous about how they might react to me, with all my bandages and burned skin. They were only babies, they couldn't understand what it all meant. So I was torn between keeping them away so they wouldn't be scared, and bringing them to the hospital so that I could see them.

When Yvonne finally did bring the girls in to see me, I was shocked at how big they were. They had grown so much in the six months that I was in the ICU. Best of all, they came right to me and didn't hold back. They were very brave.

The best days were when my daughters came to visit. Sometimes Yvonne would bring them, other times my mom and Gwen would pick them up. They would sit on a grownup's lap at first, and then after a while Monique, who was the older of the two, would come and sit by my bed.

Monique was eighteen months old now, going on two, and she had changed the most. She wasn't the little toddling baby I knew before the fire. When she was a little baby and starting to crawl, she only crawled backwards. She would turn her head and look behind her, but she couldn't see too good, so we had to move things out of her way.

Me and Yvonne laughed at that. After a while, Monique got the hang of it and crawled forward.

While I was in the Intensive Care Unit, Monique took her first steps. Yvonne told me about it. By the time I was moved to the Ward and getting up in the chair, Monique could walk all around my hospital room. She loved to feed me cookies. Cookies were her favorite food, so she naturally figured they were my favorite, too. She would take a cookie and hold it up to my mouth so I could bite it, and that made her smile.

Another thing that surprised me was how much Monique was starting to look like me. Yvonne's mother, Bernice, saw the resemblance, too, so she put one of my old hats on Monique, a Tigers baseball cap. She was wearing it when she visited me in the hospital.

One day when I was in therapy, Yvonne brought Monique to see me. Monique gave me a piece of candy. As I took it in my mouth, she told me, "Say thank you."

That was the first time I heard her talk. That lifted my spirits so much. I was so proud of her for learning to speak, like she was the first child in the world to do it. I was proud of Yvonne, too, for how she was raising our daughters. I wished I could be home with them and watch every new step and hear every new word, but at least I was comforted knowing she was growing and learning so well.

Kim was only two months old when I was burned, so she didn't know me very well at all. By now she was not yet a year old, but she still spent most of her time in somebody's arms. She was a quiet baby. She didn't fuss a lot. She always seemed to have a smile on her face.

Both the girls seemed okay being with me, even though I still had a lot of bandages on my arms and legs and chest, and even though my face was so torn up and discolored. I didn't have any eyelashes or eyebrows. No ears, either. But Monique and Kim didn't cry or seem scared when they saw me, which was a big relief for me. I'd look at the girls and I'd be happy. It's hard to describe. I loved them so much, and I wanted so much for them to be happy and well raised. Pretty clothes for church, a nice home, a good school.

I didn't know how I was ever going to get back to working in the auto plant and provide for my family. That made my daughters' visits bittersweet. I was happy to see them and sad to think what the future might hold: poverty and welfare, or their growing up with another man that they called "daddy."

On days when my daughters didn't get out to visit me my sister Gwen would come in by herself. She would talk about her friends; she was fourteen years old and just starting to go out with boys. She would ask me about boys, especially what I thought about the guy she was dating. She would ask, and then she would listen. She thought I had a good judgement.

I asked her if she could bring me a record player. Gwen brought in a little 45 player with the fat spindle you load the records on. It would play them one right after the other, so I was still able to listen to my Motown favorites. Regina Reno, Nate, Pug, and June all brought records up for me to listen to.

As I got stronger my mom started to lose the fear that I was going to die. Where my dad provided the strength to sit up with me all night in the Intensive Care Unit and help with my dressing changes in the tank, my mom brought the nurturing and companionship that I needed for this part of my recovery.

She would sit and talk about the family, the neighborhood, my Uncle Pearlie and Aunt Pauline. She still brought in her home cooking; her biscuits didn't give off steam when she cut them open, but they were just as fresh and tasty as when the came right out of the oven. It was like being home in the kitchen hanging out with her. We adapted to our circumstances the same way you accept a stretch of bad weather on the farm.

My mom cooked for me every week. I didn't have to eat hardly any hospital food, she brought so much good down home cooking in for me. There were fresh vegetables from the garden, especially her greens. I loved her greens. The black-eyed peas were cooked down so they were soft and easy for me to chew. And there were sweets, too, like her banana pudding. That was my favorite, it was so easy going down.

She was always a woman of quiet strength and unspoken dignity. Her gentle voice and easy laughter were always a lift for me. She was the forgiving opposite to my father's stern discipline. Ever since I was a child, I depended on her for solace, and I depended on her now. The strength of her love combined with the nourishment of her cooking made a powerful healing potion. On days when she was there, my gloomy thoughts were chased away, and I believed I was going to get better.

As the spring turned to summer, my room got really hot and humid. The Intensive Care Unit had air conditioning, but not the ward.

When you get hot, you sweat. The water on your skin evaporates, and it carries away heat with it, leaving you cooler. But my sweat glands were burned away. I was in danger of suffering heat stroke, because my body couldn't cool itself down in the hot room.

My dad brought in a fan, which helped a lot. Lying in that Circle Electric bed in the summer, I felt like I was back at my grandfather's farm in Silverdale picking tobacco. Sometimes it even seemed as hot as the barn when grandpa had the oven roaring and he was curing those tobacco leaves till they were golden brown.

My dad was still coming to look after me after he got off of work at midnight, though now he wasn't coming every night, since I was doing so much better. He would sit for just a couple of hours, then he'd go home and get a little sleep. In the morning, he and Uncle Treetop would come back again, so that they could help lift me into the tank for my dressing change.

I still needed to go to the tank every day for my dressing changes. They didn't have as much staff on the Ward as they did in the Intensive Care Unit. As a result, it was harder to get someone to take me to the tank, especially on the weekend.

A lot of the time Uncle Treetop and my dad helped the orderly take me to the tank. If not for them, I would have missed a lot of my treatments. They would lift me up and lower me into the whirlpool nice and gently. The water still had salt in it, and it burned like fire. I'd see the nurse pour that can of Morton salt into the water, and I knew it was going to be bad. It was just like the way they salted meat to keep it from spoiling, only they were salting me.

My dad and Uncle Treetop even helped remove the dressings. It took a lot of guts to work with the doctor and the nurse and deal with the blood and my injuries, but my dad and Uncle were tough. They always saw to it that I got the care that I needed. And they didn't complain to the staff about it, either. They never said, "What's wrong with you? Why can't you care for our boy?" They just picked me up and took me for my treatment.

By this time, Yvonne didn't visit me too often. I could see that she was still in a daze, like she couldn't believe what was happening. She was only eighteen, it wasn't like she'd been out and seen the world. She was still in shock over my injuries, not to mention having to raise our daughters by herself.

Among the family members and friends who visited me, some

were better at hiding their fears than others. Like Ball and my dad, and Nate—they kept their poker faces so as not to make me worry. But Yvonne didn't play poker, and she couldn't hide her fears from me.

My sister Gwen was still in high school, and she started bringing a girlfriend of hers over to see me in the hospital. The girl's name was Pat. Pat came to see me so often, people in the hospital started calling her my wife. I had to explain that she was just a friend, there was nothing more to it.

Pat was comfortable around sick people. After she graduated from high school she went to school for inhalation therapy. She just felt at home taking care of people in the hospital who needed her. She liked to take care of them. But most important, Pat saw past my injuries. She was able to talk to me just like she would have done before I was hurt.

Her visits really boosted my spirits. We would joke and tell stories and talk about anything at all. When school was out for the summer she wouldn't miss a single day visiting me in the hospital. I grew very fond of Pat, although I was still married and I expected to go back to living with Yvonne once I recovered from the burns.

Getting a visit from Gwen and Pat, or my friend Napoleon or Rodney Reno or Preacher, they were what I looked forward to the most. It was like Christmas morning every time somebody I knew came in through the door.

But then there were the hours and the days when nobody visited me. When you're lying flat on your back on the Circle Electric Bed, all alone, what can you do to pass the time? I listened to sports on the radio. My dad brought me a radio, and whatever game was playing, I listened to it. I didn't care who was playing or what sport it was: baseball, basketball, soccer. Even tennis. Or golf. I even listened to wrestling! College or pro, I was into it, and it kept me going. Following sports really held me together.

After I was on the ward for a month or two, the Social Worker, Miss Klein, got a special deal for a television that I didn't have to pay for. Following the teams gave me something to focus on. It kept me from dwelling on myself and feeling sorry for myself.

I had a roommate, an older guy, around thirty-five, named John. He was being treated for a gunshot wound to his stomach. His wife had shot him. John told me, "One thing I got out of her shooting me was, my wife really loves me."

"Say what? What do you mean she loves you?"

Delbert McCoy

I never did find out exactly what John meant. He was a light-hearted sort of guy. He worked in the auto plant, like I did, and he didn't take too many things seriously. Which was surprising, considering the fact that he had a colostomy. But the colostomy didn't seem to bother him, it was only temporary, and his marriage was for life. That was John's view, anyway.

I thought that was kind of strange. Maybe his wife found him fooling around, he never said. Maybe he was trying to cheer me up.

Of course, baseball was the sport I liked the best. I *had* to listen to my Tigers. When I was in high school I dreamed of playing for the Tigers. My couch said I had a shot at making the team. Now I listened to every one of their games, and I followed every play.

The year before, in 1968, the Tigers won the World Series. Denny McLain, their ace pitcher, won 31 games. He was the last Major League pitcher to win 30 games in a season. Most people didn't give the Tigers a chance to do it again in 1969. They started their year slow, with more losses than wins, but I still hoped they would come back. As July heated up, their bats cooled down. The Baltimore Orioles were leading them by 14 games.

One game, on July 14, the coach scratched Denny McClain, their ace pitcher and team captain, and put him on the disabled list. Denny had circulation problems in his arm. With him out of the rotation the Tigers lost their top pitcher.

Mickey Lolitch pitched in place of McClain against Baltimore. He struck out ten batters. He was awesome. Then, with Norm Cash getting on base, Jim Northrup came up to the plate. Ernie Harwell was the announcer; he was the voice of the Tigers. When Northrup hit a fastball, Ernie called it, "That ball is going...going...it's out of here, a home run!" That put the Tigers ahead by one run. Pat Dobson came in to relieve Mickey in the ninth inning, and they held the lead, beating their fiercest rivals.

The victory made me happy all day. It was a bad break for the Tigers to lose Denny McClain to the disabled list, but they had other strong pitchers who could take up the slack. I still had faith in my home team. Somehow my faith in the team helped me keep up my faith in the doctors and my chances for recovery. As long as the Tigers had a chance to make it to the playoffs, no matter how slim it was, I was sure that I had a chance, too.

If there was no sports playing on the radio or the TV, I could look at the newspaper, so long as I was on my stomach or sitting up in the chair. If I was lying on my back, I couldn't sit up properly; the Circle Electric didn't flex at the head like a true hospital bed, and that made reading the paper difficult. All I could do was listen to the radio and hope somebody came in to keep me company.

Eventually, Nurse Pfeiffer would come in. "It's time to flip you," she'd say.

Flip me. It sounded like I was a pancake or a fried egg. She fastened the second mattress on top of me, strapped in my arms and legs, then she tightened a leather strap holding my head down. My forehead itched from the scar tissue, and I always rubbed my forehead against that leather strap. I rubbed that strap so hard I wore through it and they had to get another one.

Nurse Pfeiffer pressed the button on a control box, and I was turning upside down again, the astronaut, until I was lying on my stomach. Once I was lying on my stomach, she laid the newspaper out on the floor and I could read it. I would study the tables and statistics. I even had a lot of them memorized. Even though I couldn't go out to see a game live, I knew more about what the teams and the players were doing than almost anybody.

When I'd finished reading two pages I had to wait for a visitor or one of the nurses to turn the page for me. Lucky for me, there were a lot of statistics on the sports pages. That made them last longer. I would read those numbers over and over again, comparing different players and teams, thinking about who would win in today's game based on what the individual players had done before. I hadn't given up on the Tigers. Neither had my dad, though Napoleon and Luther had written them off a long way back. They were sixteen games out of first place, and their ace pitcher, Denny McClain, was hurt.

But I always rooted for my home team. I believed they wouldn't let me down.

Sometimes listening to sports didn't take my mind off my troubles. I would get down in the dumps and not want to get out of bed. Dr. Grifka gave orders for the nurses to get me up and walk in the hall. It was important if I was ever going to get my strength back to exercise. All of my joints were locking up. If I didn't work them they would freeze permanently. Then I'd be in even worse shape than I already was.

But it was hard to keep going day after day, with the heat and the boredom and the pain of the dressing changes. Some days I just couldn't get myself to follow Doctor Grifka's orders. Even Mr. Johnson couldn't get me out of bed. He would tell me it was "Doctor's orders" and he wasn't in any mood to play, but I stood my ground and wouldn't get up.

I just couldn't see the point of making myself hurt worse when I was never going to get better. I didn't believe I was ever going to play ball again in the alley behind my house, or dance in Shorty's basement, or take my own wife, the mother of my two daughters, out for a drive in a car. Or hold my two baby girls in my arms and swing them around and make them giggle and smile.

On those really bad days my brother Luther was the only one who could get me out of bed. Ball never took any crap from anybody. He was tough and he was persistent. He would come into my room, pull a chair up, straddle the chair and put his face up close to mine.

"What's this I hear you telling the nurse you're not getting up today?" he'd say.

"Ah, Ball, I'm worn out. Don't make me get up."

"Now look. You been through the fire, you died and come back, and it didn't happen for no reason. You have to get up, and you're getting up. Let's go."

I'd look into his determined face and know there was no good arguing with Ball. He meant business. He'd grab me around the chest and pull me up into a sitting position. Then he'd take my arm and ease me onto my feet.

I leaned against my brother, took a step. The physical therapist had started me walking, but my ankles were weak and could hardly hold me up. If my ankle turned, the way it sometimes would, Ball would catch me and hold me up. He didn't need any special belt or parallel bars to support me, he was strong and determined, just like my dad. Out in the hall we'd go, me bobbing up and down on account of my joints were stiff, Ball holding me and encouraging me.

"Thatta boy, Delray. That's it. Keep going. Just a little bit farther."

When we finally got back to my room after it seemed like I'd walked a hundred miles I'd want to get back in the bed, but Luther would ease me into the chair.

"You're not getting back to bed," he'd say. "Don't even think about it. You need to be up more."

I'd sit up, he would prop the newspaper in my lap, and I'd read the sports section all the way through, every line and every word. As long as I was in the chair, I could tease the pages over with my hand, or I'd push the paper up to my face and turn them with my mouth, which was better than having to call somebody in to do it.

I was a different person than the Delco who was full of energy, gathering the guys to play a ballgame, even in the snow. I didn't think I could ever be that kind of person again. I didn't have any idea who I was anymore.

Maybe my dad was right. Maybe God did have a reason for me surviving when the doctors thought I wouldn't make it, and my heart stopped three different times. But if He had a plan for me I couldn't see what it was. I didn't see how I could ever become a useful, worthwhile human being. How could I earn a living and support my family? How could I be a father to my children and a husband to my wife?

I only saw more pain and operations ahead of me, with no end of them in sight.

CHAPTER NINETEEN

As 1969 came to a close, Dr. Grifka came in and told me he would like to transfer me to a first class burn unit at St. Joseph Mercy Hospital in Ann Arbor, Michigan. It was pretty far from my home, a good fifty miles, which would make it tough for my family to visit. Dr. Grifka said that the team there was the best in the country. If he could get me in there the trip would be worth it.

But there was a problem. My Blue Cross insurance was only good for a year, and it was going to run out at the end of January, 1970. I had the Blue Cross insurance from my job at Chevrolet Gear and Axle. It covered a stay in any hospital for up to one year, but no longer. When the twelfth month was over, they would stop paying and the hospital would discharge me, even though I was still very sick and needed a lot more surgery.

My second job was at Chrysler. That job also gave me insurance. It was a plan called CHA. CHA was under the jurisdiction of the United Auto Workers union. That plan required that I be treated in a hospital that had a contract with the union. In the Detroit area, the only hospital that the CHA approved was Metropolitan.

Dr. Grifka thought he'd be able to convince Blue Cross to start my coverage back up, but it was going to take some time. In the meantime, the CHA plan wouldn't pay for me to stay at Detroit General Hospital. I was going to have to transfer to Metropolitan Hospital.

I asked Dr. Grifka how long he thought I'd have to stay at Metropolitan. He said it would be "for little while."

I asked him what he meant by "a little while." Dr. Grifka said he wasn't sure. It could be a couple of weeks. It could be longer.

"What was Metropolitan Hospital like?" I asked.

"They aren't up to our standards," he told me. "They don't have our residents, so they're not up on the latest techniques."

Then Dr. Grifka took my dad aside, where I couldn't hear. Years later I learned that he told my dad that the doctors at Metropolitan were not very good with burn victims like me, and he should watch what they did. They didn't understand burns the way the doctors at Detroit General did. He also asked my dad to keep in touch with him and let him know how I was doing.

I didn't like what Dr. Grifka told me about the other hospital, but I didn't have any choice in the matter. The insurance company

103

was calling the shots. I just hoped that Dr. Grifka would work out the deal to send me to St. Joseph Mercy in Ann Arbor as soon as possible.

In January, 1970, as my insurance ran out, Dr. Grifka did a final skin graft. The graft took good; that was encouraging. Dr. Grifka was afraid that the doctors and nurses at Metropolitan wouldn't know how to care for the graft, and the graft would die. He fought as hard as he could to keep me at Detroit General, but the insurance company won the fight, and they sent me to the union hospital.

It was hard leaving my friends at Detroit General. After a year in their care, that was what they were to me: friends. I cried when they called up the ambulance to take me out. Some of the staff cried, too. Marlene and Miss Pfeifer and the Social Worker Sharon Klein all cried and wished me well. They put on brave faces and told me I would be fine, and I shouldn't worry, but I was still plenty scared.

Marlene tried the hardest to cheer me up. She told me I'd be okay, that Dr. Grifka would get me into St. Joseph real soon. But I could see the concern in her eyes. She was afraid for me because she knew the care at Metropolitan wasn't as good as at Detroit General.

The ambulance came, the paramedics loaded me into onto a stretcher, and pretty soon we were traveling across town to Metropolitan at Woodrow Wilson and Tuxedo.

As soon as I got inside the hospital I could tell it was a big step down from where I'd been. The walls and the floors were old, the paint was peeling, and even the lights were kind of dim. There didn't seem to be as many people working there as I was used to at Detroit General.

The people were nice, they welcomed me and got me settled into bed. I was scared. I didn't know if they would give me my medicine or help me with my food. I didn't know who would change my dressing, or take me to the tank for my daily soaks.

On the second day at Metropolitan, the doctor in charge of me, Dr. Romano, pulled off the last skin graft that Dr. Grifka had given me. I don't know why he took it off. I knew from all of the surgeries that if the graft didn't take, it had to be removed, but this one seemed to be doing okay. It didn't make any sense to me.

Dr. Romano didn't replace the skin graft with a new one, either. He covered the wound with dressings and left it wrapped up tight. He wasn't anything like Dr. Grifka. He didn't call all over the country trying to get skin grafts. I didn't hear him talk about harvesting cadavers. It seemed to me like, as soon as they took a look at me, they just gave up. Like I was a hopeless case.

That night I started to bleed from where he took away the graft. Soon the dressing was wet with blood. The blood ran out from under the bandage and into the bed. It looked like I was bleeding as bad as when I first arrived at Detroit General the night that I was burned.

I got really scared. I thought I was going to bleed to death. I called out, "Nurse! Doctor! Help me, I'm bleeding!"

The nurse came in and saw all the blood, and she got scared, too. She called Dr. Romano. It seemed like things went from bad to worse. Dr. Romano got the bleeding stopped by wrapping a new dressing over me extra tight. But there was no talk of rushing me in to surgery for a new graft. From that day on, it seemed they didn't hardly want to treat my wounds at all.

At Detroit General I was going to surgery once or twice a week, but at Metropolitan I only seemed to go that many times in a month. I got several transfusions, because it looked like I was bleeding more than I did before. The whole healing process slowed. It even went backwards.

Not only did the surgeries nearly stop, but it was hard for me to get to the whirlpool treatments, too. Metropolitan didn't seem to have as many nurses and nursing assistants as Detroit General. It was hard to get someone to take me to the whirlpool, where they could soak away the old bandages. My dad and Uncle Treetop offered to take me to the Physical Therapy department themselves and put me in the tank. They explained how they had taken on a lot of my care in the past.

But the staff at Metropolitan wasn't as willing to let my family be responsible for my care. They said that *they* had to do it, even though a lot of the time that meant that it never got done. The hours would pass, and still nobody took me down for my treatment. Finally, the nurse would come in and tell me the physical therapy department was closed, it was too late, and I would have to wait until the next day to get to the tub.

All in all, it was a gloomy place. Most of the staff cared about me and the other patients, but I could see there weren't happy with the place, either. If they were down in the dumps, they couldn't do much to keep *my* spirits up. I found myself losing faith. Losing hope.

I even lost a lot of my interest in sports. Nate would bring me the Daily News, but I didn't read the sports section page by page the way I did at Detroit General. The Red Wings were playing. Normally I would be listening to the game and cheering for Gordie Howe and the rest of The Production Line to score a goal. But my heart wasn't in it. I was too down. It looked to me like I was never going to get out of Metropolitan Hospital alive.

I had fevers off and on almost every night. My wounds were bleeding more and more. I was losing weight and my legs were getting so stiff I could hardly walk. On top of that, the nurses didn't make me exercise like they did back at Detroit General. My condition was going down and down.

One night Dr. Romano called my house and told my dad that he should come down to the hospital right away. "I've done all that I can do," the doctor told my dad on the phone. "I don't think your son will be alive in the morning. You better come down tonight."

When my mom and dad came, the doctor told them again that he had done everything he knew how to do, but it didn't seem like it was enough. My dad got very upset with him. He told Dr. Romano that I had survived a year at Detroit General, when they didn't give me more than a thousand-to-one chance of making it, so how was it that ever since I came to Metropolitan, my condition was getting worse and worse?

At that point Dr. Romano called another doctor, Dr. Feller, at the Burn Unit in St. Joseph Mercy Hospital, in Ann Arbor. Dr. Feller gave him some suggestions for my treatment. They gave me a transfusion, and I felt a little better, but not much.

I turned to God. I prayed to God to help me get back to Detroit General Hospital and Dr. Grifka and Marlene. I asked him to return me to people I trusted and who wanted me to live. I prayed to get me to St. Joseph Mercy Hospital in Ann Arbor, where they had the number one burn unit.

I prayed and asked the Lord to please not let me die.

CHAPTER TWENTY

After three months in Metropolitan Hospital I was losing my strength and losing hope. My wounds were bleeding more than they had since I was sent out of the Intensive Care Unit at Detroit General. My dad talked to the doctors, and he and Uncle Pearlie offered to help with my whirlpool treatments and my dressing changes. But even with their help I was getting worse and worse.

My spirit was leaking out of me along with my blood. I could hardy talk or move around in bed. I didn't want to eat. I didn't have the strength to sit up or exercise. I didn't even care about watching sports on television. Everyone in the family was getting more and more upset. They wanted to know why my condition was deteriorating.

My mom and dad called Dr. Grifka and told him how bad things were. That I was going down and down, and that I couldn't hold out much longer.

Dr. Grifka kept calling every day to Ann Arbor. He was talking to Dr. Irwin Feller, who was in charge of the burn unit at St. Joseph Mercy Hospital. It was very difficult to get the insurance company to cover a transfer to a better hospital. There was a lot of red tape, a lot of "maybe's" and "we'll see's." But Dr. Grifka never gave up.

On top of the problems with the insurance companies, there wasn't any bed open in the Burn Unit at St. Joseph. They didn't come up very often. Doctors all around the Midwest wanted to get their patients in Dr. Feller's Unit, it was known all over the country. Patients were flown in from hundreds of miles away to be cared for by Dr. Feller and his staff.

My condition got so bad that I could hardly sit up and eat, or even talk. The doctors at Metropolitan acted like I was a terminal patient. It was as if they threw up their hands and gave up on me. Things were almost as bad as when I was first burned and arrived in the ambulance at Detroit General Hospital a whole year before.

My dad called Dr. Grifka early on Saturday morning and told him it was now or never. "If you can't get him in St. Joseph, he's not gonna make it."

Dr. Grifka told my dad to stay by the phone, he would call Ann Arbor and get right back to him.

Miraculously, a bed was open at St. Joe. On top of that, I had passed a grace period required by Blue Cross to be readmitted. The insurance company agreed to pay for a stay in another hospital. The only catch was, they weren't willing to pay for the ambulance to get me there.

My dad didn't wait another minute. Even though it was early on a Saturday morning, he called the ambulance company himself. He made the arrangements for them to pick me up at Metropolitan Hospital right away, with him paying cash on the spot for the trip to Ann Arbor.

A little while later the paramedics came to my room. They loaded me on the stretcher and took me away before Dr. Romano and the nurses even knew what was going on. If anybody on the staff objected, my dad told them it was all arranged by Dr. Grifka, that the burn unit at St. Joseph was ready.

I was out of there before anybody could blink an eye.

June drove my dad and mom to St. Joseph Mercy Hospital in Ann Arbor. They got lost on the way, and that made them worry. They knew that I was in very bad shape; they remembered the night that the paramedics carried me from the Soul Expression to Detroit General. They were afraid I would die on the trip and they would never get to see me alive again.

By the time they found the hospital, Dr. Feller had me in the Burn Unit and hooked up to an intravenous. He scheduled me for a skin graft right away. Dr. Feller had spoken with Dr. Grifka, so he knew exactly what needed to be done, and he started working on me as soon as I got in the bed.

Like so much of my story, I didn't learn the whole truth about the day I transferred out of Metropolitan Hospital until many years later. It turned out that when my dad and June and mom arrived at St. Joe, Dr. Feller told them that if I had got to the hospital a half hour later, he would have had to send me to the morgue instead of the burn unit, I was that close to death.

From day one at St. Joe I knew that I was in a first class hospital with the best staff in the world. They started with skin grafts. Soon Dr. Feller added the whirlpool treatments for my dressings changes. After that, he began physical therapy, and after that, occupational therapy.

He was a lot like my dad, Dr. Feller was. Strict. In charge. There was *his* way and there was no other way; his way was how everybody did it. Maybe he had been in the military, too, but if he was, I never heard about it. At first, he seemed kind of mean. I had to do exactly what he told me to do, no getting off easy, and no compromise.

It didn't take me long to see that, just like my dad's way of raising us kids was best for us, Dr. Feller's tough program was what I needed to get better. I had a lot of problems. My joints were all locked up. I couldn't open my hands, couldn't bend my elbow to touch my nose, couldn't walk more than a couple of steps. Plus, I still had several open wounds that needed skin grafting and antibiotic ointment and whirlpool therapy.

Dr. Feller made it clear that I had to get with the program if I was going to stay in St. Joseph, so that was what I did. When the doctor told the nurses to get me up out of bed, I got up. If I told the nurses I didn't want to get out of bed, they would call Dr. Feller, and he'd come down and talk to me and then get me up himself.

He was a short man, kind of chunky, with salt and pepper hair, and glasses. He always wore a fine suit, and always acted like a real gentleman. He had a dark complexion, which made me think he might be Greek, although Feller isn't a Greek name. He had a very precise way of talking, too. He was obviously very well educated, but at the same time he never talked down to me or to any of the nurses or the young doctors in training. He explained what the plan was, and he made sure everybody followed orders.

He worked with a partner, Dr. Kathy Richards. She was quite different from Dr. Feller. Dr. Richards meant what she said, too, but she would joke with me, where Dr. Feller was always serious. She would get a laugh out of me, tell me how good I was doing, and make me smile, even when I was hurting.

Dr. Richards was a short woman, medium build, with short brown hair. Her lab coat was too big on her, so it hung over her wrists and down onto her hips, like a little girl who borrowed her mother's clothes. At first, I wasn't sure she was as strong a doctor as Dr. Feller, but soon I learned that she was a terrific doctor, too, she just had a different way about her.

The physical therapists were also the best. They worked on me every day, getting me up out of bed and taking me to the whirlpool for my treatments. They didn't use salt in the water, the way they did at Detroit General Hospital and Metropolitan. They used an iodine-type solution that stung a little bit, but wasn't nearly as painful as the salt.

One of the therapists was named Rob. Rob had this long straight hair that hung down to his shoulders. He had a long face, too, and dark eyes which looked into your eyes without blinking. When you talked to Rob, it seemed like you were looking into the face of Jesus, the way he didn't blink.

Once I got used to how he looked, I had the feeling that Rob had all the time in the world for me. Like, when he listened to me, I was the most important person in his life. Rob was very religious, and we talked a lot about our faith and how much God was in our lives. He helped me through a lot of dark days with his faith.

Another physical therapist was Robbie. She was short and pretty, with very long blonde hair. Mostly she wore her hair piled up on her head, with pins and a clip. But toward the end of the week it seemed like she got tired of messing with her hair, and she let it fall down to her waist. She always had a smile for me, always upbeat and enthusiastic about how I was doing.

After about a month of skin grafts and whirlpool therapy, Dr. Feller and Dr. Richards decided to call in an orthopedic surgeon to help them try and restore use of my hands, arms, and legs. My fingers had fused together when they healed. They were more like a web hand than a human hand. You couldn't even tell where each finger ended and the next one started. My fingers were also frozen in a closed fist. I couldn't open them to grasp anything. My wrist and elbows were also locked up.

The orthopedic surgeon was named Dr. Herbertson. Dr. Herbertson was a big, powerfully built man who looked like he could play pro football. I wouldn't be surprised if he played sports in college. He had huge hands, and he seemed to take up the whole doorway when he came into my room. He also had a positive attitude. He told me he was gong to do everything in his power to restore my movements. He told me straight up that my body was in bad shape, and he wasn't sure he would be successful. It would mean a series of operations. Maybe more than twenty.

I told him I would do whatever he said, I had complete confidence in him and Dr. Feller and Dr. Richards. It was such a relief for me to be in the hands of caring people who were treating me and who at least hoped they could restore my body. They were applying all of their knowledge, calling on the whole staff to pitch in and try to make me better. I couldn't ask for more than that. The rest was up to the Lord.

I underwent over thirty operations while I was at St. Joe. They separated my fingers, and put pins in the joints. Dr. Herbertson hoped to give me some ability to open and close my hands. He also hoped to give me the ability to bend and straighten my elbows, which were frozen.

The operations on my hands didn't help very much. Too much of the muscle and connective tissue in my hands were destroyed. I got a little use of my thumb, which let me pinch something small, but I didn't have the strength to really hold something solid, like a cup of coffee. Still, just the fact that the doctors were trying to get me moving was a hundred times more professional than anything I'd seen at Metropolitan.

I had whirlpool treatments every day, even on Saturday. On Sundays, when the physical therapy department was closed, the nurses filled the tank themselves and took me down to it. Nobody had ever done that for me in Detroit.

St. Joseph Mercy Hospital was a teaching hospital, and Dr. Feller had a responsibility to teach the young doctors and students, as well as take care of patients like me. Sometimes he would take me to a lecture he was giving. He wanted the younger doctors to learn how to treat burn patients. He would take me in a wheelchair to the auditorium, pushing the chair himself.

When he introduced me, he called me his "star patient." Dr. Feller put slides up to show the students and the doctors in training pictures of my burns, then he would explain about the treatments and the difficulties of getting wounds like mine to heal. After he finished with the slides he would show them my burned limbs, and they would ask him questions about my progress.

Some people might be uncomfortable being put in front of a crowd of doctors and students, but I didn't mind it much. I knew that I was helping them learn to be doctors, and I thought that maybe by studying me, they'd be able to take better care of another burn victim when they were admitted into the hospital.

Once in a while Dr. Feller would send me to the University Hospital, where the doctors there could see me and learn about my case. He had his slides with him, and the audience was even bigger than the one at St. Joe, the University being a major medical center.

With so many dedicated people working to make me better, I began to think that I might really recover. Not just that my burns would heal, but that I might get a little use of my body. I knew I would never play baseball again, but maybe after all the operations I'd be able to hold a ball in my hand. Or write my name on a piece of paper.

Maybe I could pick up my daughters and hug them, and hold my wife's hand in mine.

While I was on the Burn Unit I had a special treat that really lifted my spirits. One of the nurses knew that Willie Horton was my favorite Tigers ballplayer, because he graduated from my high school, Northwestern, and because he was a black man who came up from a poor section in Detroit. The nurse called the Tigers and told Willie about me. Willie got the whole Tigers ball club to autograph a baseball for me, then he sent it out to me at St. Joe.

The nurse was so kind to me, the way she took time to contact the Tigers and tell Willie about me. And the team was so kind, I just couldn't believe my good fortune. That autographed baseball was like the watermelon that my dad brought to me in the Intensive Care Unit at Detroit General. It was a kind of lucky charm that I believed would help me get better. With the whole Tigers baseball team rooting for me, my spirits were lifted. I resolved to work as hard as I could and never give up on myself again.

CHAPTER TWENTY-ONE

By August I was healed enough to leave the Burn Unit and to go out to the ward. Dr. Feller transferred me to the orthopedic ward on the third floor. My problems were mostly in my joints and my lack of flexibility, not so much the open skin that bled and needed grafts. I only had a couple of open wounds on my chest and leg by this time, and they just needed daily dressing changes.

The head nurse on the ward was Miss Mary Haab. She was from the old school of nursing, just like Dr. Feller was from the old school of medicine. Miss Haab was great. She was strict and loving at the same time, like the best parts of my dad and my mom. She wore a wide nurse's cap with a point on the top and a starched uniform. She had this warm smile, and she would talk tough. Just like when I was back on my grandfather's farm, there was no getting out of my chores.

"Delbert," she'd say, looking at me sternly, "today you have to ambulate the whole way down to the end of the ward and back!"

The nurses used a lot of hospital talk that I didn't always understand, like telling me to "ambulate," but when Miss Haab put a pair of slippers on my feet and a bathrobe around my back, I knew she meant for me to start walking.

I had a walking cast on one foot because my ankle was very weak, the muscles were mostly burned away. My foot would turn in when I put my weight on it. The walking cast had a special heal that let me put weigh on it. But the leg with the cast was longer than the other leg, so when I walked, I bobbed up and down like somebody with one shoe on and one shoe off.

The ward was laid out down a long straight corridor. Going the length of the hall and back was a good distance for me, and I didn't want to do it, but I knew that if I didn't to it, Miss Haab would call Dr. Feller, and then I'd really be in for it.

The nurses saw that I was shy about being out in front of people. I had a lot of scars and discolored skin. On top of that I had no hair on my head and no ears. I looked a little like a freak, and I was afraid that the other patients and their visitors would stare at me, so I tried to stay in my room all the time.

When I did go out in the hall, usually, the other patients and visitors were polite and didn't stare at me. But every once in a while, somebody would do or say something that really cut into my heart.

One time in October a man was visiting somebody, and when he saw me he said, "Well, I guess you won't need a mask for Halloween." I think he meant it to be funny, I don't think he meant it to be mean, but those words made me feel bad for a long time.

Miss Haab could be tough when I needed a strong hand, and comforting when she saw that I was losing my hope. She knew it pained me to be seen in public. Even so, she knew I needed to get over my fear of being seen. She stuck a chair out in the hall and made me get up out of bed, walk out into the hall, and sit there all morning long. The nurse's aide brought me my meal in the hall, and I had to eat it there, too.

Believe it or not, in those days hospitals allowed patients to smoke. I would sit in the hall and ask one of the aides, "Will you light me a cigarette?" I couldn't hold it in my hand, so the aide had to put it up to my mouth.

I knew they were busy, so I didn't ask too often. When it looked like somebody was free, I'd ask for the cigarette. Each time they struck the match in front of my face, it made me jump. I'd pull real hard on the cigarette, smoking it kind of fast because I hated to take up too much of the aide's time.

Dr. Feller helped me get over my shyness, as well as my injuries. One day, he asked me would I go down and talk to another patient who had been burned. The doctor knew that most of the time I had a very positive outlook. Even though I was limited physically, I was very strong, spiritually. I believed I had a future and that things would work out for the best.

I went to the burn unit and talked to a patient named Gus. Gus was in a motorcycle accident. He was burned over 30-40% of his body. His burns were on his legs, his stomach, and his hands. The burns were on top of the abrasions where the skin was torn away. He was the worst of the burn patients while I was in Saint Joe.

I didn't say much. Mostly, I sat and listened to Gus. He told me about the day he was in the accident. He told me about his family and his job. Once he got to talking, he told me about how he was afraid he wasn't going to make it.

Gus was afraid of the same things I was afraid of. He asked me what kept me going, why I didn't give up and die. I told him I felt like giving up plenty of times, starting from the day I was burned over a year ago. My heart had stopped three different times; you couldn't get any closer to dying than that. But my family was there for me every day—that gave me strength. On top of that I felt that God had a purpose for not taking me. I told Gus about the vision I had the first time my heart stopped.

"It seems like there's something the Lord wants me to do on earth," I told him. "Otherwise he would have taken me, just like in the vision.

I don't know if Gus was encouraged by my story. He was in a lot of pain, and he was scared half to death. But Dr. Feller encouraged me to keep on visiting him, and so I went to the unit as often as the nurses could take me.

My first roommate on the burn unit at St. Joe was Steve. He was an electrician who got burned on a pole. The electric current went down his arm and out his leg. He lost his leg, and his arm was in very bad shape. Dr. Feller wasn't sure he was going to be able to save the arm. One night I woke up and I saw blood spurting from his arm. I pushed the button and called out, "Nurse! Nurse! Get in here, Steve's bleeding!"

They rushed him to the operating room and had to amputate the arm. After that, Steve was very down. He didn't want to eat or talk or see his family. He was giving up.

I told Steve, "Look at me: I can't use my hands, I can barely walk, but *I'm* not giving up. I have a lot to live for, and so do you."

We talked about God and our family, and about what made life worth living. I told him that I still expected to raise my daughters. Maybe I couldn't do all the things that a father should do, but I could still tell them right from wrong. I could sill help them with their homework. Tell them stories. Support them. I told him that being there for my family was the thing that got me through my long, terrible nights in the Intensive Care Unit back in Detroit, and they got me through now, too.

I think that my talking to Steve helped him a little, because he gradually got more active. He went to physical therapy and occupational therapy. They fitted him with an artificial leg. By the time he was discharged, he was more independent than he ever imagined he could be.

Steve and I watched a lot of sports on the TV. It was hockey season and the Red Wings were hot that winter. Two of the nurses were big Red Wings fans. Whenever we had the game on, the nurses would run in and ask us, "What's the score? Did Gordie make a point?"

Gordie Howe was the star of a great team. He played with Frank Mahovlitch, Pete Stemkowski, and Garry Unger. Three of their best players, Gordie Howe, Sid Abel and Alex Devecchio, were called "The Production Line," after the auto plants. They had an exciting year. Me and Steve got so excited rooting for the Red Wings we would forget we were in the hospital. The nurses came and stood in the doorway to watch for a few minutes, then they would have to get back to work. It was almost like being at home in the family room.

There was a lot of love on the Ward at St. Joseph. The whole staff adopted me. They couldn't do enough to make me comfortable, just like the nurses and doctors did in Detroit General Hospital. They knew that I was a pretty good distance from my home, which made it hard for my family to visit. That made them work even harder at making me feel at home.

Miss Tarpley was an old nurse's aide. She was from a farm down south, like my mom and dad were. Miss Tarpley was lean and strong. Her muscles were as tough as turkey gristle. She could pick me up and lift me into a chair all by herself, but most of the time she made me stand up and move myself around.

My skin was dry because most of the glands that produce oil were burned away. When the skin grew back, the glands didn't come back very much. As a result, my skin was always itching, which drove me crazy. Miss Tarpley would spread cocoa butter on my back and chest. I would tell her, "Rub harder Miss Tarpley, rub that skin right off!"

She would rub the butter in until my itching was gone, and then she would tell me it reminded her of spreading bag balm on the udders of her cows. I knew about bag balm from my childhood summers down in Silverdale. I told her about the summers I used to spend on Grandpa McCoy's farm; she told me about how she grew up on a farm. We had a great time swapping stories about the pigs and mules and all the kinds of work that had to be done.

Sometimes Miss Tarpley or one of the nurses would take my clothes home and wash them and iron them for me. She would bring them back all clean-smelling and neatly folded. All of the staff were like that, doing extra things to make me feel at home.

Among the occupational therapists, Martha was especially kind and encouraging. She was a quiet woman, very devout. We shared a strong faith, and she encouraged me to trust in God and believe that I would get well. We prayed together sometimes; that always made me

Delbert McCoy

feel stronger and more determined to get better.

Robbie, another one of the occupational therapists, tried to help me do more for myself by attaching a spoon and a fork to a pair of leather wrist straps. With the utensils strapped to my wrists I could just about feed myself. My arms didn't bend at the elbow very far, so I had to lean forward and shovel the food up to my mouth. I maybe wasn't the neatest person in the world, but it sure felt good to be able to do a little for myself. I may have made a mess, but I was happy.

In the Spring, Dr. Feller made some decisions. He had hoped that the orthopedic surgery Dr. Herbertson did would give my joints flexibility. But the pins they put in my hands didn't help, I still couldn't open and close my hands. My hands were still locked in fists, and my elbows still had hardly any flexibility in them. I still couldn't touch my nose with my fingertip, my joints were so stiff.

Seeing how my hands were so limited in their function, Dr. Feller asked Dr. Herbertson if he could do an operation that would allow me to press my thumb and forefinger together. "We'll give him a pinch," he suggested. "It'll be just enough to allow him to hold a pencil or a utensil."

Dr. Herbertson took me to surgery and fixed my hand so that I got my pinch. That was all I was going to be able to do with my hand: squeeze my thumb and finger together and bring food to my mouth.

At least my hips and legs were doing pretty good. I could get up into a sitting position without too much help. But my ankles were weak. The walking cast made it possible for me to walk a little, but as soon as the cast was removed, my ankle turned in and wouldn't take my weight.

My hands couldn't hold on to a cane or a walker, so there wasn't any help for me that way. I was very limited in my walking. I could go the length of the hall and back, and that was about it. If I wanted to go further, like to the gift shop, I had to go in a wheelchair.

The good news was, my skin was doing a whole lot better. Almost all of my wounds were closed. I only had a couple of patches of open skin on my chest. The skin on my face and back was wrinkled up with folds, called keloids. I also had all these patches of my body that were different colors. Some were real dark brown, others were pink. The keloids were ugly, and the pink patches looked strange against the chocolate brown.

I didn't see my family as often as when I was at Detroit Gen-

117

eral or Metropolitan. My dad came out as much as he could. So did my brothers and friends. But Yvonne and the girls didn't come like they used to. That weighed on my mind. I was getting better, which meant I was getting closer to the day I could go home. I just didn't know what home would be like. I didn't have any idea how I could be the husband and father that my family needed.

As much as I was hopeful and happy at my progress, the fate of my family weighed on me. There were decisions to be made about where I would live. Would Yvonne be able to take me in and care for me along with the children? My family life was up in the air, like a game that was suspended on account of the rain. I wasn't sure if I was going to be brought back into the game.

CHAPTER TWENTY-TWO

The week before Christmas, 1970, when Dr. Feller and Dr. Richards made their morning rounds, Dr. Feller said to me, "Delbert, how would you like to go home for the holidays?"

Between my stay at Detroit General, Metropolitan and St. Joe, I'd been in the hospital continuously for nearly two years. I was terribly homesick. The staff at St. Joe worked really hard to make me feel like I was part of their family, and I did feel like I belonged. But even with all of their good-hearted efforts, Dr. Feller could see that being away from home for another Christmas really got me down, and that I wanted to be home with my family.

Except...

Except for one nagging fear that I couldn't get out of my mind. My body was changed. I looked bad. Ugly. I wasn't sure how people I had known for years would act when they saw me. Would they see the same old Delbert, or would they see somebody completely different? A stranger? A creepy guy they didn't want around?

Sometimes the words of that visitor at St. Joe came back to haunt me: "I guess you won't need a mask for Halloween." Those words still sent a chill down my spine every time I remembered them. The fear of old friends turning their back on me gnawed at my heart. A couple of times I even told my mom and dad that maybe I shouldn't come home when I was released from the hospital.

"What are you talking about?" my dad said. "You belong home with us."

Still, I worried about how people would react to me. When I told Napoleon about how I felt, he said, "Man, you're the same Delbert Ray you always were. Everybody can see that in five seconds. If somebody doesn't like how you look, don't pay them any mind. Ignore them."

This wouldn't be the first time I was allowed out of the hospital. Once, during the summer, George, one of the St. Joe security guards, took me to his house in Chelsea for the day. He lived with his wife and son right on a lake. He carried me out to his car, carried me into his house, and he even put me on his boat. But Dr. Feller's proposal was even better than a day in the country.

"When can I go?" I asked him.

"How about today?" he said. "But it will only be for a day or two. You still have open areas that need dressing changes, and you still need daily physical therapy."

I got right on the phone and called my house. Two of my brothers, June and Ball, came out to the hospital to get me. Rodney Reno came, too. They rode out in June's car. He had 1969 Cadillac. A hard top. They picked me up just after lunch and drove me to my dad's party store.

Detroit looked different to me. I had been away for almost two years, so maybe it was my memory that was fooling me, but the streets seemed different to me. They looked smaller, darker, not as well lit. The city seemed poorer to me somehow, and weighed down with sadness.

I had never seen my dad's store. It was on the first floor of a two-story building, with four apartments above it. The store was on Chicago and Grand River. The store had a big neon sign on the front, Al and Mae's Party Store. I really liked the sound of that name.

My dad came out. He stood by the car and we chatted a while. He was telling me how glad he was that I'd decided to come home on the furlough. He was worried that I might not come home when I was discharged; that I might go south, because it was so hard for me to face my family and friends, with all the scarring and being so disabled. I had faith in my close friends, like Nate and Rodney Reno, but I wasn't sure about other people that I knew.

After my dad went back into the store, we stopped at Cunningham's pharmacy, like we used to do. Luther got me a Daily News to read. I wanted to check the sports scores. Then June drove us home. There was snow on the ground, but no one was playing baseball in the alley behind the house.

When I first got in my home I was tired from the trip and the excitement, so I sat around and watched TV. I read the paper some more and talked with everybody. My mom and Gwen and Jackie cooked their hearts out that holiday. My Aunt Pauline, Uncle Treetop's wife, was in the kitchen, too. My dad was busy at the store. He and my brothers were spending a lot of time there, because Christmas was a make-or-break time for a business like theirs.

When my father and Uncle Treetop got home around seven PM we ate supper. Father always said grace. He still does it, even to this day, when we have a big family gathering.

After dinner we all sat around talking about things, just being a family. Dad told me some more about the party store. He was happy.

Uncle Treetop was helping out at the store. So were my brothers. It was a lot like life down South, where everyone pitched in and helped make the business a success.

He told me about things that had happened while I was away. There was a lot to fill me in. Gwen and Jackie were still in school and living at home. We sat around talking. Napoleon came over, Rodney, a lot of the guys, Preacher, and Pug (Lamont Lawrence). We talked and laughed. I smoked a cigarette and had a beer, just one, and relaxed, I was just so glad to be home.

We watched TV and talked some more. Some of my friends went out to finish their Christmas shopping, then they came back and hung out some more. It felt good to be home. It felt safe. Everyone accepted me the way I was. Nobody seemed bothered at all by my appearance; nobody seemed to mind helping me with things I couldn't do myself, like lighting a cigarette or pouring a glass of beer. Being surrounded by my family and my good friends made it the best Christmas I could ever have imagined.

All the guys slept over. They slept on the floor in the living room while I slept on the couch. I didn't want to have to deal with the stairs, I still had the walking cast on, and stairs were really hard; I couldn't hold on to the banister.

In the morning mom and the girls made a big country breakfast. Pancakes and sausage and biscuits, grits with lots of butter, bacon, scrambled eggs. It was a feast.

All through the day the guys came and went. They left to take care of business, there were last minute gifts to buy, it was coming up to Christmas, but then they came back and hung out some more.

I had dressings that needed to be changed, so Luther did them. My dad and Uncle Treetop could have done it, but Ball stepped up and took charge, like he always did. Nothing scared Ball, and nobody could stop him once he made up his mind.

He changed the dressings on my back and my chest. He spread the silver nitrate solution and wrapped the gauze around me, just as neat as any doctor ever did.

It was no surprise that Ball would take charge of my care. When I was at Detroit General and I wouldn't walk for the orderlies or the doctors, Ball was the first who would say, "I'll get him up. He'll walk for me. "

Ball would come into my room, pull a chair up close to the bed, and look me square in the eyes.

"You got to get up and walk," he'd say. "You don't want your bones to get stiff. The doctor said you have to do it and you're gonna do it. Let's go."

I'd let him take me by the arm and get up, and I'd hobble down the hallway. He was a tough guy, my brother Ball, and tender at the same time.

When evening came, Napoleon called me on the phone. He said, "You want me to drive you over to Yvonne's mother's, don't you?"

"Yeah, sure," I said. I had two doll babies for the girls that Jackie and Gwen had bought. I couldn't shop, so they went out and bought them for Monique and Kim when they heard that I was coming home.

Napoleon knew that I had the gifts for my daughters, but now I was getting that scared feeling again. I was going out and meeting people; I wasn't sure how they would accept me. I was especially scared about how my daughters would react.

"Yeah, I guess I should go," I said, dragging my feet. I didn't want to give up the safety of my home and my family.

"I'll be there in ten minutes he said," and hung up.

Around six o'clock Nate pulled up in his car. He and Lamont Lawrence carried me out to the car, I still couldn't walk too good, especially with steps and the ice and snow outside. I had the gifts for the girls tucked in the crook of my arm. They helped me into the passenger seat. Napoleon wanted to bring a bit of Christmas cheer to Yvonne's family, so he put an unopened bottle of brandy in the back seat. It was Martel cognac.

Nate put the car in gear, and we were off, just like old times, like we'd done a hundred times before.

We were going down Dexter. I was talking about what I was going to say to Monique and Kim. Suddenly, we saw a flashing red light behind us. It was a police car; they were pulling us over.

We were at Joy and Dexter in a rough section of town. It was just a block from the Marathon gas station where Robinson and Kelley had borrowed the can of gasoline to set fire to the Soul Expression, and just two blocks from the scene of the fire. Just the fact that we were driving by that place made me nervous. Now, with the police car behind us, I was getting more anxious by the minute.

We weren't far from Yvonne's mother's house, so I was hoping the police would let us get on our way soon. Napoleon rolled down his window and asked the cop what was the matter.

"You got a busted tail light," the cop told him.

"Oh," said Nate, "I'm sorry, I didn't realize that."

He showed the officer his license and registration.

When the cop leaned over to look at Napoleon, he saw the bottle of cognac in the back seat. As soon as he saw the bottle, the cop ordered Napoleon out of the car.

"You're drunk!" he said. He didn't bother with any drunk test. Didn't order Nate to walk a straight line or stand on one foot and touch his toes. He just assumed that Nate had been drinking.

Napoleon tried to tell him that the bottle of cognac wasn't even open, but the cop wouldn't listen to him.

"I'm taking you down to the station for carrying an open bottle of liquor in the car," the cop said.

Napoleon explained that he hadn't been drinking. "I'm just taking a little Christmas cheer to my friend's wife. Look, the seal on the bottle isn't even broken!"

"Turn around, put your hands over your head!" the cop told him.

He patted Nate down, but he didn't find anything, not even a pocketknife. Then the cop handcuffed Nate with his hands behind his back, like he was a dangerous criminal.

While the first officer was arresting Napoleon, a second one got into the driver's seat. He started shining his flashlight and looking around the car. I guess he was looking for drugs. Of course, he didn't find anything. Napoleon didn't mess around with drugs.

I don't know if it was because both the cops were white and Nate and I were black, but those two officers wouldn't listen to anything that we said. They were as mean as the mule on my grandfather's farm that wanted to bite me.

Through the window I heard Nate say, "My friend is handicapped. He's on furlough from the hospital. You can see, he can't drive the car. He can't even walk."

I held up my arms and showed them that I didn't have use of my hands. I still had bandages on my head. There was even a cast on my left leg, but they didn't pay any attention to me.

"I've got to take him back home," Nate told them. "He'll freeze to death if you leave him here."

I told the second officer who was in the car, "This is where the fire happened that burned me. I'm scared to be left here alone in the dark. I can't help myself. You can't leave me here."

The second cop pulled Nate's car into an alley and turned off the engine. He left the key in the ignition.

As he got out of the car, he said to me, "Get home the best way you can," and closed the door.

He walked back to his police car, watched as the first cop put Napoleon in the back, and then he got inside and drove away.

The cop didn't radio anybody to come check on me. He didn't take down a phone number and call my family to let them know where I was. He just left me there in the alley to freeze to death.

The keys were in the ignition, but there was no way for me to drive the car. I couldn't even turn the key to start the engine so that I could stay warm, and Christmas time in Detroit is a cold time of year. Once it snows, often as not the snow doesn't melt till the Spring.

I was alone on a cold, dark night in a rough section of Detroit. There were drug dealers and prostitutes in the area, and I was scared to try and talk to just anybody. I decided to wait until I saw somebody I thought I could trust.

Now me, I was never a real heavy person. I was always lean, but since the burn, I was even skinnier than I'd ever been. There was hardly any fat on my body. Beside that, I wasn't dressed to stay out in the cold. I had a coat on, but no long johns or boots.

I was in the car for about an hour. Pretty soon I started shivering. My teeth were chattering. I was scared that I could die right there in the car.

Finally I saw a girl who looked all right to me. She had on a leather coat, a hat and boots. I knocked on the window to get her attention. The Caddy had power windows, so I couldn't lower one of them to talk to her. I couldn't open the door, either.

She saw me and stopped walking. She looked over at me. She was cautious, which was only natural, given that it was dark and the neighborhood we were in was rough.

After a minute she walked slowly over to the car. I asked her to open the door, so I could speak to her. I held up my hands so she could see that I was disabled.

She looked at me. She must have seen the fear in my eyes, because she grabbed the handle and pulled the door open.

She had guts, to open the door to a complete stranger. I didn't look like a normal guy, either. But she realized that I was cold and scared. I think it was clear to her that I would die from the cold if I didn't get help.

I told her what happened and asked her to call my wife.

"There's a pay phone just around the corner at the Marathon station," I told her. That was the very place where Kelley and Robson had bought the gasoline to start the fire. I told the girl Yvonne's number, and she went over there and called.

She spoke with Arthur Searce, Yvonne's brother. He came right over on foot, it was only a couple of blocks. He started the engine, cranked up the heater, and took me back to their house.

I was frozen all the way through my body, shivering like crazy and my teeth chattering. Yvonne wrapped me in blankets and gave me some hot coffee with lots of sugar.

As soon as my teeth stopped chattering, I asked Arthur to call the police station and find out what happened to Nate. We called to make sure we had the right station house, then we called Nate's mother. She went down to the station right away to check on Nate. She told us he was okay.

They kept Nate in jail until the morning. During the night, the cops who pulled him over changed their story. When they first arrested him they said they were taking him in for having an open bottle of liquor in the car and for being drunk. But they realized that he wasn't drunk, and the bottle of cognac wasn't even open.

Lucky for the cops Nate had some outstanding parking tickets. They kept him in jail until the morning, when his mother paid the tickets, after the motor vehicle office opened, and then they let him go.

My parents and family were very upset over how the police had treated me.

"I can't understand how a man can treat somebody like an animal," my dad said. "Like his life don't mean a thing." He had been in the Second World War and had seen a lot of brutal things, but the behavior of the cops was as mean as anything he could remember from the war.

After the holidays we got a lawyer and filed a suit against the City of Detroit and the Police Department. I already had a lawsuit against the owner of the Soul Expression and the Marathon Gas Company that owned the gas station where the arsonists bought the gasoline. I hoped that all my suits would give me enough money to buy a nice place for Yvonne and the girls and me, and help out my mom and dad, too.

125

Even though my holiday was messed up by the cops and being stranded in the cold, I still had a merry Christmas, because I saw my family and my wife and my daughters. They came over to my parents' house. Kim and Monique liked the dolls that Jackie and Gwen bought for me to give them. Best of all I was surrounded by friends who accepted me for what I was.

There was no looking away from me; no funny look on their face; no pity in their voice or horror in their eyes. There was just friendship and love and the spirit of Christmas.

That was the best Christmas I could ever have. I saw for the first time that I was still *me,* just like Napoleon had been telling me for a year. I was messed up and helpless, but I had a place where I belonged and people who loved me. Things could have been a whole lot worse.

CHAPTER TWENTY-THREE

On July 21, 1971, Dr. Feller told me I could go home to stay. My wounds were healed. The surgeons had tried their best to free my joints, from my hands and wrists, to my elbows, shoulders, hips and legs, but they had mostly failed. I was about as flexible as I was going to be. The physical therapists taught me exercises to keep the little bit of flexibility I had. Dr. Feller told me I had to get out and walk as much as my legs would allow. The rest was up to me.

Dr. Feller was very proud of me. He knew that I worked hard while I was at St. Joseph Mercy Hospital. He believed in me and in the strength of my faith. He also had faith in my family, because he saw how much they came through for me.

But the doctor did have one thing that worried him. I had taken a lot of narcotics during my two and a half years in the hospital. I wasn't getting them now, but still and all, Dr. Feller was worried that when I was out I'd get prescriptions for painkillers and become a drug addict.

I told Dr. Feller that was one thing he didn't have to worry about. I hated drugs. Ever since I tried that marijuana at Johnny's and was sick for three days, I never had any desire to put drugs in my body. I had come too far to go backwards. My heart stopped three times when I was in the Intensive Care Unit at Detroit General Hospital. I'd nearly died again when I was transferred to Metropolitan Hospital. I survived too much to let drugs poison me and cut my life short.

Besides which, my daughters needed their father with them.

My parents put together a big dinner party for me when I got home. Everyone was there: Dad and mom, June, Ball and Slow, Jackie and Gwen. Uncle Treetop and Aunt Pauline, and all my friends—Napoleon Ross, Preacher, Pug, Shorty, and lots more. Yvonne and the girls were there, too. It was a wonderful party.

My mom, my sisters and Yvonne worked all day cooking. They made all my favorite dishes: chicken and dumplings, sweet potatoes and mashed potatoes, candied carrots, greens, turnips and black-eyed peas, biscuits and fresh baked bread. We had turkey and dressing with Uncle Treetop's secret sauce. He was the best cook in the whole family, and that's saying a lot. . My mom cooked the desserts I liked the best, banana pudding and peach cobbler.

There was more food than we could eat in a month of Sundays.

We stayed up late and talked. Mamma made coffee: regular for my dad and my sisters, Sanka for her and for me. We talked about all the things we didn't have time to talk about when I was in the hospital. They asked me what I planned to do. At that point I really didn't have any idea where my future lay. I couldn't walk too good. After Dr. Herbertson took off the walking cast, the muscles in my ankles were still too weak to hold me up, and sometimes my foot turned in on my when I walked.

My left hand was completely useless. It was just a stump, really. My right hand had a little use; I could move the thumb and first finger in a pinch, and I could bend the elbow enough to get my hand to my mouth. But mostly I needed help with everything, from getting dressed to bathing.

It was a good thing I didn't have any hair on my head, there was no way I could hold a comb and reach the top.

I told my mom, "I don't have a future."

My mom said, "That's crazy, of course you have a future."

I told her, "I don't see there's much I can do. I can't even write or use a computer. There's nothing I'm good for...Nothing at all."

Mamma said, "God has plans for you, Delbert. He wouldn't let you live without him having plans for you."

My dad agreed. "You have a bright future," he told me. "You just have to find out what it is."

My sister Gwen said that I could do lots of things, I just had to go back to school and find out what I was able to do. She told me, "Delray, you are a fighter, you have never been a quitter."

A part of me wanted to go back with Yvonne and my daughters, but I couldn't take care of myself. I needed help with everything, from washing to eating to dressing myself. I even needed help going to the toilet. It was too much to ask Yvonne to take care of me and the girls; they were still babies.

Over the next couple of days I talked with Yvonne about where I was going to stay. I decided it was best if I lived with my parents, at least in the beginning, on account of I was so limited in what I could do for myself. I needed help with everything. Yvonne agreed. She had her hands full with the girls; it would be real hard on her to have to care for me, too.

Even with me living at home, I still saw Monique and Kim every week. Yvonne would bring the girls over to the house, or Gwen or Jackie would pick them up. The girls helped feed me and keep me company. That made me feel good.

Being they were still little children, their idea of a meal was cookies and potato chips. They would take turns feeding me snacks like that. I guess they figured that if they liked the food, it must be the best food in the world, so I let them give them to me.

I liked to read to them. They would sit on either side of me holding a book, and when I paused, Monique would turn the page for me. They learned to help me with little things that most people take for granted. They could hold a tissue up to my nose so I could blow it. They could hold a cup for me to drink, then wipe my mouth with a napkin.

It didn't seem strange to them that their daddy needed help. Children are like that. They accept things. My daughters accepted the change in my abilities, and they pitched in, just as my brothers and sisters and I had always pitched in to help our family out.

My dad was busy with the party store, so he was gone all day and into the evening. That left me home with my mom and my sister, Gwen. It gave us time to get closer. We spent hours and hours in the kitchen drinking coffee and just talking about things. My mom would get out the jar of Maxwell house instant coffee. She'd make mine with two sugars and cream, and a donut or a biscuit on the side. It was like the family picked right up where we left off the day before I went to the Soul Expression two and a half years ago.

I was still the third son of six brothers and sisters. Still the one who loved sports and followed the Tigers with my dad. Maybe I couldn't do a lot physically, but mentally and emotionally, I had the same special place in my family that nobody else could fill.

I spent a lot of time that summer watching the Tigers on TV or listening to them on the radio. My dad and my brothers watched the All Star Game with me. It was held at Tiger Stadium that year. The All Star Game was always a special thing for us. Vida Blue was pitching for the American League against Dock Ellis for Pittsburgh and the National League. Sparky Anderson managed the National League. He was managing the Cincinnati Reds. He put in Willie Mays for the leadoff batter and centerfield. It was Willie's 22nd All-star Game.

There were four Tigers on the All-Star team: Al Kaline, Mickey Lolich, Norm Cash and Bill Freehan. Mickey won 25 games that year, he was a great pitcher, but Vida Blue got the start.

I was rooting for the American League Team, Detroit being an

American League town, and we were down three, nothing, when they put in Reggie Jackson to hit for Vida Blue. Reggie was playing for Oakland that year. He was just starting out on his career, and he was only in the game because he was replacing an injured player.

With a man on first, Reggie came up to the plate. Dock Ellis threw nothing but fastballs, and he was throwing for strikes, too. I could hear the "thump!" every time the ball hit the catcher's mitt.

It was a one ball, two strike count on Reggie. The announcer described the windup, then, all of a sudden I heard a loud "*crack*!" Reggie had connected. We could all tell from the sound that the ball was gone.

The announcer called out, "This ball is going...going...It's gone....Wait a minute, folks, I think it's hit the light tower on the roof! I've never seen a ball hit that hard at Tiger Stadium!"

I was so happy that day. The American League was winning, and Reggie had jacked that ball into history! I was watching baseball with my dad and my brothers back in my own home.

It really seemed like old times.

CHAPTER TWENTY-FOUR

After I was home for a while, life settled into a routine. I needed help with everything, from feeding to dressing to bathing. I couldn't cook for myself, so I depended on people for that. My whole family pitched in, adding my needs to the daily chores of going to school and work and whatever else needed to be done.

It might seem surprising to some people how natural it was for everyone in the family to take care of me, but it didn't surprise me at all. Partly, I think it was because my parents grew up poor on a farm, and that was how farm people were. You expected tragedies to happen. When somebody got hurt or was crippled or they died, somebody else, a cousin or a neighbor, would just pick up the slack and do what they had to do to keep the family going.

You shared the bounty of the harvest and you shared the burdens of bad years. You didn't take advantage of your neighbor or relation when they hit a rough time; you helped them out as best you could, knowing it would be your turn one day, because you knew that sorrow was coming one way or another.

The other thing that held our family together was our faith. When we were kids my mom and dad made sure we went to church and Sunday school. My dad said grace before the evening meal, and all of us said it with him. Our faith bound us together and held us up when we were discouraged. My parents trusted that God had a plan for each one of us. I maybe didn't always see things with the same conviction that they had, but I had faith. So did my brothers and sisters, and our faith kept us going.

We believed that God would judge us by our deeds. I grew up believing that it's more important to put something into the community than it is to take from it. That's why I was a union steward at Chrysler, so that I could help my co-workers with their problems. Now I was the one on the receiving end, and it was hard to accept that.

That was really my biggest problem, that I wasn't a giver, I was a taker. I couldn't support my family, and that made me feel really bad. My check from social security was only $183 a month. When I had the two jobs at the auto plants, I was taking home more than double that amount in a *week*. Now, here I was getting just so much in a whole month. There was no way I could support my family on that little bit of money.

So I had to get used to depending on my mom and dad and brothers and sisters, just like when I was a little kid. Everybody made adjustments and kept on with their lives. My dad went to the Party Store every day. My brothers helped out at the store. Jackie was in school, but she helped out in the store, too. Gwen was finishing high school, so she and my mom were home with me most of the time.

I needed help with everything. Even washing myself and getting dressed. I had that pride about not wanting my mother to care for me, so I relied on Nate and my brothers to help me. They would wash me up and get my clothes on me.

I tried to do for myself. I even made a point of walking down the stairs alone. But Dr. Feller warned me the ankle might give out any time, and sure enough, it did. I went tumbling down the stairs. After that, we put my bed on the first floor and I slept there.

Now that I was out of the hospital, Yvonne visited me a lot more, and we mostly got along. She was patient and good to me. We joked and talked. Most of the time it seemed things were getting back the way they used to be between us. Other times, June or Ball would drive me over to Yvonne's; she was staying with her mom, Bernice. I'd stay overnight and visit with the girls.

Monique was turning five, and she liked to help me. So did Kim. They liked to help put my shoes on. Kim wasn't yet four, and she wasn't good with tying laces, so she helped squeeze my feet into my shoes and Monique tied the laces. They would both smile and giggle. It tickled them to death that they were helping their daddy.

I was comfortable at home with my family and at my mother-in-law's with my wife and daughters. But I wasn't comfortable going out in public. It didn't feel safe. Napoleon and Ball wanted me to get out of the house. They kept bugging me to go out with them, but I wasn't ready to show my face out in public. They saw I was getting depressed staying in all the time. They knew that if I was ever going to develop self-confidence I had to face going out in the world. If I didn't I would wither away.

One day Nate came by in his car. He said, "Let me take you outside. You can't stay in the house all the time."

"I don't want to go," I told him. "People will stare at me."

Nate said, "We're your friends. We look at you like you're the same old Delbert. Folks that look different, they don't matter. Forget them."

Delbert McCoy

I began to get that fear, like when it was time to go for my dressing change. But Ball wouldn't take no for an answer; he never did. He and Nate carried me out to June's car–he drove a Cadillac–even though I kicked and hollered and complained a whole lot. June drove us to a club downtown. They helped me walk into the club. I sure wasn't going to let anybody carry me into a bar.

We sat and ordered a beer and talked. We smoked some cigarettes. I was nervous and kept my head down. I had a hat on to hide my bald head, and I didn't take my jacket off. Every once in a while I sneaked a look around the club, and I was surprised to find that nobody was staring at me. Nobody said anything about how I looked. Everybody minded their own business and didn't bother me or my friends.

We talked and sipped our beer. The longer we talked, the more I relaxed. Every once in a while I would steal another glance around the club. Nobody even noticed I was there. I didn't catch anybody pointing at our table and whispering something about me. They just minded their own business.

When we got up to go, Napoleon took my arm, my ankle was still weak and it gave out on me without warning. The bartender told us to come back again real soon, and we left.

It was great! "Y'all come back real soon," was what the bartender said. I believed him. I was ready to go back the next day and have another beer.

Once Nate and Ball and June got me out in public, I started to believe that I could do something useful, and not just sit around at home and drink coffee. It was a slow process, it didn't happen overnight. But little by little I got up the nerve to be out with people. The more I got out in public, the more confidence I developed. That helped me begin to think about what were my options and how was I going to earn some money for my family.

My dad asked me to work for him in the party store. Everybody else in the family was helping out, and I didn't want to feel like I wasn't doing my share. Uncle Treetop was working part-time at the store, and one morning he came and picked me up. He was the right man to do it, too, he was always such a positive guy. My dad was right, he was always just as happy as a bird in a tree.

At the store you needed somebody to watch the door so nobody walked out with the merchandise. I could do that all right, my eyes were good enough for that, although they still didn't close all the way. I'd get infections in them from dust that got in, because I always

133

slept with my eyes partly open. But even with the eye infections, I could see well enough to keep an eye on the door.

After working in the store for a while, my dad put me on the counter at the cash register. That was a real challenge for me. My left hand didn't open at all, it was no more useful than a stump, and my right thumb and first finger only moved a little bit in a pinch.

I set up the money at the start of the day. The bills were in their slots in the cash drawer. I arranged the coins in neat rows on the countertop. I could hold a pencil with an eraser on the end in my right hand. When somebody paid for an item, I put the customer's bill in the drawer, and I pulled out the smaller bills with the eraser on the end of the pencil. Then I'd slide the correct coin change across the counter. The customer only had to pick up his change from the counter and the sale was made.

Just like the first time I went to the club with Ball and June and Nate, I was nervous dealing directly with the public. Not being as quick with the change as my dad or Uncle Treetop, I was afraid some customers would get angry having to wait. But people were accepting of me. They didn't complain or make any nasty comments about my limitations. For the most part people took me as I was. I think they were glad to see somebody with my disabilities working and trying to help myself. Not a few of them told me so, and that made me feel good.

Most of all I felt good to be working. I didn't make very much money, but at least I was contributing to my family, plus I was getting out of the house every day. That gave my mom a break. She was starting to look a little worn out.

CHAPTER TWENTY-FIVE

The winter of 1973-74 was a cold one, with a lot of snow that piled up on the sidewalks and wouldn't melt under the weak Michigan sun. Detroit was in a deep freeze, and so was the economy. The Big Three car companies, GM, Ford, and Chrysler, were in a slump. There was a gasoline shortage in the summer, and a lot of people were buying small foreign cars instead of the big, gas-hogging ones that were made in the Motor City.

Slumping car sales meant more layoffs in the auto plants. More layoffs meant the economy was icing up. People in Detroit were put out of work by the thousands. As a result, they spent less money on food and clothing and everything else. The whole city was going into a depression, both mental and economic. There was more poverty. More hopelessness. More drugs.

More crime.

In January, 1974, I was helping out at my dad's Party Store. We also had a cousin working with us, Clifford Riley. Clifford wasn't a true cousin, but he was very close to our family, so we called him one. Me and him were friends from the time I was two years old growing up in the Northwestern section of Detroit.

Clifford loved basketball the way I loved baseball. He played it all the time. He was six foot ten inches tall, and real skinny, which got him the nickname Slim-T. He played for the Western High School team. He was a big star on the team. He had a room full of trophies, and was always in the local papers. The pro teams scouted him. Everyone said he was going to make it as a professional basketball player.

After finishing high school Slim-T served in Viet Nam. When he was discharged he came back to Detroit to work on his basketball. He expected to win a tryout with a pro team any day.

I was living at home with my mom and Gwen. Gwen was working at the Detroit Bank and Trust—it's called Comerica, now—and going to Wayne State university. Things were going good at the Party Store. People in Detroit still celebrated Christmas that year, even though it was hard times for a lot of them, so we had a good Christmas.

On the evening of January nineteenth, a Saturday, I fell asleep in the dining room on the couch. The phone rang, waking me up. It was dark outside, around 8 o'clock at night. My sister Gwen answered the phone, just like she did the night that I was burned.

Gwen listened to what the caller had to say without saying a word, then she hung up. She looked at me. Her face was frozen. I could see the fear in her eyes.

Gwen told me, "The man on the phone said they took Ball and Cliff. They've been kidnapped. They're going to the Party Store. They want twenty thousand dollars to let them go."

At that time there was a vicious gang operating in Detroit, and they were terrorizing the city. They kidnapped people, broke into houses, raped women, and murdered people. They spread fear across the city.

It came out later how the gang operated. Ball and Clifford had just left their house. The kidnappers followed them in their car. They pretended to be police, with a siren and a flashing light on their car. They ran the light and siren and pulled Ball over. Next thing, the criminals pulled out their guns and took them away in their car.

We also learned later that one of the kidnappers knew Ball slightly. They weren't friends, they just had a mutual acquaintance. Ball drove a Caddy. My dad and June had Cadillacs, too, so the kidnappers thought they had a lot of money.

Gwen called over to the Party Store and told my dad. I stood beside her at the phone. We didn't want mom to know, so we kept quiet, but she overheard us calling the store, anyway.

"*What's wrong? What's wrong?*" she asked us. From the look on our faces, she knew it was very bad news.

Gwen tried not to tell her, but eventually she broke down. She cried and told her, "Ball and Clifford are kidnapped!"

I called June, who was home at his apartment. He rushed right over to the store. As soon my dad heard what happened, he called in the police. He was willing to pay the kidnappers, although he didn't have that kind of money around at night. I guess he could borrow the money from the bank with a loan against the store, although that would take time, especially with it being Saturday night, and we didn't think we had much time with this vicious gang holding Ball and Clifford.

The police came to the Party store. They drove up in regular police cars, not unmarked cars. We were afraid that the kidnappers would see the cops and get scared, and then they would kill Ball and Clifford, but it was too late to do anything about it.

The police came to the house, too, again, in regular marked cars. They told us to sit and wait for another call to come in. We did what they told us.

My dad and June stayed by the phone at the store. The more the time passed, the more scared we became. But the kidnappers didn't call back. Not to the house, and not to the store.

Ball was engaged to a sweet girl by the name of Brenda Colvin. He had a son named Derron and a step-daughter named Rena. They all lived together, making a home and planning on having more kids after they were married.

I called Brenda. I told her I had something to tell her, that I was coming right over. I didn't go into what happened on the phone. I felt it was better to tell her in person. More humane.

An old friend of mine, Raymond, was over at the house. We called him Red Dog. Red Dog had a car. He offered to drive me over to Brenda's. At the same time, we thought we'd drive around the neighborhood and see if we could spot something. Just as we walked out of the house, I saw a car drive by the house slow. There were three young black men in the car. They were looking at our house, with the police cars parked in the street right out front.

I didn't know if those guys were the kidnappers, and to this day I still don't know if it was them. I only know that they took a long look at our house, and that we definitely didn't know them. As I looked at the men in the car, they drove away.

We drove over to Brenda's. She was the kind of girl who always had a smile on her face. She was kind to everyone. Just a nice, loving young woman. She had Ball's little boy, Derron, who was just a toddler, pulling at her bathrobe, and a daughter, Rena, who was a little older.

I told her what happened. Right away, she began to panic. She cried and cried; there was no stopping the tears. I tried to comfort her. I asked, "Do you have anything to drink?"

She had a couple of beers in the fridge, so Red Dog, Brenda and I went back to the kitchen, drank a beer, and talked. I told her not to think the worst, there was hope. We had to trust in God and believe that Clifford and Ball would be returned to us safe and sound.

After she got calm, I told her we had to get back to the house. I warned Brenda to lock her doors and not to open them for anybody unless she was sure they were the police. I was afraid the kidnappers might come for her, too.

Ray and I went back to my house. My dad was still at the store. He wanted to be there in case the kidnappers called over there.

He stayed at the store until three in the morning, but he never got a call.

The kidnappers didn't call the house, either. Nobody got any sleep that night, we were all so anxious to find out if Ball and Clifford were all right. The gang didn't send a note. They didn't contact anyone else in the family or anyone who knew us. Even if we could come up with the money right away, we had no way of telling them we would pay.

The next morning, around eleven, the phone rang. This time my mom picked it up. It was the police. They found the body of a young black man at Columbus and Grand River. He was shot in the back of the head, execution style. They were pretty sure it was Clifford's body, because the dead man was so tall. Right away, Clifford's family positively identified the body.

When she heard the news, my mom began to cry. "My son is dead," she said. "I know it, my son is dead. I can see it. I see his face staring at me, and his eyes are open but they don't see anything!"

We all tried to tell her that Ball *wasn't* dead, that there was still hope the kidnappers were holding him for the money, but she wouldn't listen to us.

"He's dead, Ball is dead!" she kept crying. We couldn't convince her otherwise.

Three or four hours later, the phone rang again. We all jumped. Nobody wanted to answer it. My dad went to the phone and picked it up.

It wasn't the kidnappers, it was the police. They found a second body in a vacant house on Brighton and Chicago, a black man in his twenties, shot in the back of the head.

It was Ball.

The police figured that they killed Clifford first, waited about six hours, and then they killed my brother.

Our family was in shock. We had been through a lot of fear and worry over my injuries. Just as thing were back to something like normal, it seemed like the sun had gone out forever on our family. We were frozen, unable to move or think.

My dad took charge, like he always did. June helped, he being the oldest. They made the arrangements for the funeral. They helped Brenda and her family arrange for Clifford's burial, too.

Because it was a murder case, Ball and Clifford had to have autopsies. They were done by the Detroit Medical Examiner. It was obvious to the police how they died, but they needed an official report, so the city took the bodies and did the post mortems, then they turned them over to the funeral home.

We held a double funeral. The viewing was at the Thompson's Funeral Home. The Funeral Home was packed with people, shoulder to shoulder, with tears and weeping and prayers for their young souls.

We knew that our Oakland Baptist Church was too small for the funeral, there being two big families with a lot of friends planning to attend. We decided to hold the service at my grandmother's church, the Unity Baptist Church. That was the church where Mr. Kinkannon worshipped. He was the father who donated skin from his dying son so that I could get through the first month of my injuries. One of Mr. Kinkannon's surviving sons was a minister at the Unity Baptist Church.

When we held the service, Reverend Kinkannon came and spoke to us personally. He told us that he knew there were several young people who knew and loved Clifford and Ball, and that we would have a lot of bitterness and anger in our hearts.

Then he said, "I know that this is very hard for you, but you must not think of revenge. I know that many of you have thoughts of violence, but do not let this hatred harden your hearts. Let God take care of justice."

There were over a hundred people at the funeral. The coffins of the two young men were placed side by side. The coffins were left open. They looked peaceful in their best clothes, their beautiful faces looking up to Heaven and their heads resting on soft satin pillows. There were giant bouquets of flowers all around the coffins.

I had taken ill after the kidnapping. My dad had to have me admitted to St. Joseph Mercy Hospital in Ann Arbor. I had an operation to remove kidney stones, and was away when they planned the service and the funeral, but there was no way I was going to miss my brother's last rites. Nate and Preacher picked me up from my hospital bed and drove me from the hospital right to the funeral.

A good while later, the whole story of the kidnapping came out. It seems that they took Clifford out and killed him right away, because somebody in the gang didn't like him. We never found out exactly why.

After the gang killed Clifford, they told Luther what they had done. Luther told them that they might as well kill him, too, because if he ever found out who killed his friend, he was coming after them. That was just like Ball. He never took any crap from anybody.

After he told the kidnappers what he was going to do, Luther's blindfold slipped. He got a pretty good look at a couple of them. They killed him because he would have been able to identify the kidnappers. Luther even told them he would identify them if they let him go.

Ball always was a tough sort of guy. He wasn't mean or violent or anything like that. He didn't start fights or carry a gun. He was a very well-behaved man. He was just the kind of guy who didn't take being pushed around from anybody. Except his dad, of course. He didn't talk back to his dad, not even when he was grown.

The way the police caught the gang was, somebody saw a man breaking into a house. He was going in through a window. The witness called the police. While the police were on the way, the guy raped a woman in the house. The cops came and caught the guy red-handed.

The police and the District Attorney wanted to put the gang away real bad. These animals had been running around Detroit raping and killing and stealing and kidnapping people for a long time. The District Attorney offered the guy a deal if he would dime on his buddies.

He sang like a canary. He turned in the whole gang.

Two of the gang were picked up in Texas. The others were arrested in different parts of the country. There were eight or nine of them in all. The trial was held in the summer of 1975. They were all found guilty of murdering Luther and Clifford, and they were all given mandatory life.

All of us in the family were crushed by Ball's death. We were never the same family again. For a long time after that we weren't able to just sit around and joke and relax. We lived day to day, like prisoners. A day didn't go by that we didn't think of the night that Luther and Clifford were taken from us.

We had all worked hard making the party store a success. It didn't make us rich. We didn't live a life of luxury. And now a bunch of thugs had decided that they could take Luther and Clifford. We would have gladly given them every penny we had if they would return those two young men to us, but they never gave us the chance.

After I was burned in the fire my mom was scared for a long time that she was going to lose me. My injuries were so frightening to her that she couldn't visit me much for the first few months I was in the hospital. The ups and downs of my illness put her emotions through a roller-coaster ride. She suffered through my first skin grafts and my cardiac arrests. My heart stopped three times; once when my dad was sitting with me.

With Ball's murder, my mother's heart was broken. She never recovered. His death changed her. It was the start of a long, slow decline. The grief took away her strength and her gladness of spirit. The strong country woman who always kept a positive attitude and a table full of food, even during hard times, was fading, never to be seen again.

I knew in my heart that her grief would someday kill her, although I never allowed these worries to come out. I never spoke them out loud, or even said them to myself. But deep down, I knew, it was the beginning of the end for her.

CHAPTER TWENTY-SIX

Month by month, with small steps, our family got back on its feet. None of us ever got over Ball's death completely. We all had days where the memories would flood over us. Mother would cry and go lie down, I would get real down in the dumps and think life wasn't worth living. My dad didn't talk about it, that wasn't his way, but I could see he was hurting inside.

My dad bought a house just outside of Detroit, in Oak Park. By then, all of my brothers and Jackie had moved out, leaving me and Gwen at home with our parents. Gwen married a really great guy, Tyrone Lee, in October, 1974. Their wedding cheered up the family. It was one of the few moments when my mother's spirits really came back. Gwen and Tyrone lived with us, too, and Tyrone helped out a lot. He was a solid, loving addition to the family.

I loved my family, and I was glad to be home with my mother while she was so down with grief. But I still wanted Yvonne and me to live together and raise our daughters, like we were doing before the fire. I never gave up on that dream.

My daughters were growing up; they weren't babies anymore. Monique was six, and Kim was five. I saw them a lot, but seeing them wasn't the same as raising them. I wanted to be there every day and be a real father for them.

Yvonne and I decided we should give our marriage one more chance. We got a flat on Strapmore on the west side of Detroit in 1976. The apartment had stairs that I had to walk up, which was difficult, my legs being weak. But Dr. Feller always told me I needed to exercise, and now I had to do it every day just to get in the door.

Yvonne was working at the S&H Green Stamps Company, I was helping out at the Party Store, and the girls were in school. We were busy all the time, which was good, because keeping busy kept us from worrying about our future. Or so we thought.

In the beginning Yvonne and I got along pretty good. We had our ups and downs, like any couple would, but we usually managed to work them out. Yvonne had a lot of responsibilities, getting me to work and getting the girls to school. That put a lot of pressure on her.

Although we tried to work out our problems, there was tension between us that seemed to grow and grow. We had been living apart sever since I was burned, which was seven years ago. Not only that, but I was a different person than the happy, confident young man that she married. I was dependent on people, and that made me get down in the dumps sometimes. I could be moody, and that wasn't the Delbert she first fell in love with.

Yvonne was different, too. When she married me she was a young girl, just sixteen. She was in high school; I was only a couple of months out of school myself. Now she was a woman of twenty-five who was used to being a single mother. Instead of having two children to take care of, she had two kids and a disabled husband. Instead of making all the decisions for her family, now she had to talk about them with me.

She married a man who was going to take care of *her*. Who bought her things and took her out and treated her right, like she deserved. Having a husband who needed more care than a baby just wasn't part of the marriage agreement. She never expected to be in that kind of a relationship, and it was hard on her. Very hard.

Some women are comfortable taking care of sick people and invalids. My mom and my sister Gwen are like that, and so is Tony. I'm like that. But I felt that Yvonne wasn't cut out for that kind of life. Having me to take care of along with two children was a terrible strain on her.

We tried to focus on raising our daughters and watching them grow. Seeing them change almost every day was like watching a magic show. They were so different, too, and as they grew, their differences grew along with them.

As a baby, Monique was more business-like than Kim. More serious. She was a take charge kind of child, a lot like Ball had been. Maybe it was because she was the oldest, although the girls were very close in age. Almost twins. Yvonne dressed them alike, in the same colors. She "twinned them out," as my dad used to say.

Monique was a hard worker as a child, and she stayed that way even today. She worked all through high school, and she's working as a lawyer full time job with the city of Detroit.

Now Kim, she just smiled all the time. She always seemed to have a big grin on here face. Kim was more playful than Monique. She loved to listen to music and to dance. In that respect, she took after her Uncle June and her Aunt Jackie.

When Kim was in high she always had a job on the weekends, and when she went to college she worked full time. She finished her degree in accounting, got a job with the city of Detroit, and is working there today.

When it was just the two girls with their mom or with me, they got along fine. But when Monique's friends came over, that made Kim mad, because Monique didn't play with her, she stuck with her friends. She was the oldest, so she naturally had older playmates.

When Kim was left out of her sister's game, she would pout. She could really put on a face. She wasn't the kind to start a fight, she just pouted. Kim would come to us for comfort, especially to her mother.

After a while each girl started to favor one of us. For some reason, Monique spent more time with me than Kim did. Maybe it was because she was older, which meant she was more able to help me with my day-to-day needs more easily than Kim could.

Partly it was because Kim was just more fun-loving than Monique. Kim was less interested in working, and caring for me was work. Hard work, sometimes. So Kim spent more time with her mother, who could play with her.

As they grew up, Monique was always closer to me, and Kim was closer to her mother. Yvonne and I didn't treat them differently. We were careful to give them the same attention and love, but kids bond differently. When I was a kid, Ball was closer to my mom than the other brothers were, even though she never played favorites. He was simply the kind of child who wanted to take care of his mother more than the rest of us did, so he and mom were very close.

Yvonne was a wonderful mother. She watched over the girls like a mother hen. She was very protective. Very loving. They couldn't go out without her or another adult with them, usually my sister Gwen or my mom. Yvonne was very strict about that.

My legs weren't strong enough for me to walk the girls to school, so Yvonne took them. She would walk over to school again in the afternoon and pick them up. She was very protective of the girls. I loved the way she watched over her girls, even while I knew that she wasn't happy having to also watch over me.

People came into the Party Store a lot and said, "You all should open a record shop. We have to go a long way out of the neighborhood to buy records."

My lawyer was telling me that I would soon be getting money for my two lawsuits. One lawsuit was against the Soul Expression for the fire; the second was against the Police Department for the two cops who abandoned me in the car when they arrested Napoleon right before Christmas. Yvonne and I talked. We decided to open a record store. The money would give us an income and an investment for our future.

My dad knew about running a store, so we could learn a lot from him. Napoleon had worked in the entertainment business. He was a DJ and manager at Hurley's Club in the Northfield Marriot, where he organized parties. Nate would help pick out the records, and maybe even get some of the local groups to make appearances.

There was an abandoned store right next to my dad's party store. It was run down and needed work, but it was small, just the right size for a record shop. I located some used shelves and glass displays that were available cheap. I found a contractor who would gut the room and put in new walls for a reasonable fee. I checked into a wholesale shop, Simpson's. There was a guy there who would sell me the records that I wanted. We decided to go ahead and open the store.

Soon after we opened the Record Shop the settlement for the fire at the Soul Expression came in. After seven years from when my lawyer first filed the lawsuit, I was given just $42,000. Half of the money went to the lawyer, so I ended up with only $21,000. That was what I received for losing my youth, my health, for undergoing over sixty operations, and staying in the hospital for two and a half years.

It turned out that the guy who ran the Soul Expression had only $10,000 in liability insurance. That money was split six ways among the worst burn victims. I only got $1600 from the insurance company. The building was not up to code, so my lawyer won more money from the owner and his insurance company.

My lawyer tried to sue the oil company that owned the gas station where Robinson and Kelley bought the gasoline. The oil company, Marathon, had millions of dollars. I figured that when we won a suit against them, I'd be in good shape, money-wise. But in 1968, a year after the Detroit riots and a year before my injury, the Michigan legislature passed a law that limited the oil company's liabilities for fires there were set with gasoline. The Michigan statehouse was a' ways run by the auto and oil companies, and when they wante' protect what was theirs, they usually got their way.

We took part of the money from the settlement to ex' store and make it into a real boutique. In addition to the 8-t' record albums, singles, and cassettes, we sold costume ' items, perfume, cologne, and aromatic oils. We sold so' scarves, too. We called the place McCoy's Records and Boutique Shop. The store looked great.

I did the office work, keeping the inventory and paying the bills. I helped out at the register when we needed, too, pushing the coins across the counter and sliding the bills out of the drawer, like I did when I worked at my dad's Party Store. The customers would tell me what music they were interested in, and I'd talk about it with Nate before I ordered it.

I had a friend we called Boomerang who worked part-time behind the counter. We grew up together. As a kid, he was a really happy, positive kind of guy. But in 1975 he was shot in the back. It left him paralyzed from the waist down. It also left him depressed most of the time. He never got back to his happy, upbeat way. When he was in rehab, Nate and I used to go down to visit him.

Once Boomerang (his real name was Terry) completed his rehab, he worked behind the counter at my store. He could handle the money no problem, but he couldn't handle the paralysis. Nate and I would take him out to a club sometimes, trying to cheer him up. I tried to talk to him about his condition. It helped for a while, but he always fell back into the depression. After a while, he quit the Record Store, and it got harder and harder to get him to come out with us.

The first couple of years, the store made pretty good money. We joined with my dad and the Party Store to make some radio ads. That brought in more customers. I was happy more than words could say, because I was earning a living again and supporting my family. There was nothing in the world that mattered more to me than being a provider.

In addition to helping pick out the records for the store, Napoleon was working at the Northfield Marriott Hotel. He was a Manager and DJ at Hurley's Club in the hotel. Customers would sometimes ask him about what sports team to bet on. When they did, Napoleon would call me—— he didn't know much about sports—and I'd tell him who was the favorite, what pitcher had the better record against which team, and that sort of thing. Nate made some pretty good money recommending bets to his customers, because when they won, they gave him a good sized tip. He would call and thank me because his customers were winning, and it was all because of my studying the sports pages or years.

Napoleon was the MC for the bands. He had to keep the audience entertained between the acts, and so he came up with a trivia game. It was based on sports. Nate offered any couple a free dinner and a night at the hotel if they could answer an obscure question about a major sport.

There were two problems with his trivia game. First, he really didn't know a whole lot about sports. He never followed it the way that I did. Most of what he knew, he learned from me and some of my friends.

The second problem was that Napoleon's boss didn't know about the game. The hotel never approved the free dinner and the free night at the hotel. Nate couldn't afford for anybody to ever win, because if they won, he'd have to go to his boss and tell him about what he gave away.

I was worried that somebody would get the answer right, and Nate would be out of a job, so I suggested that he make it a two-part or even three-part question. That would make it harder for the people in the audience to get the whole question correct.

Every week Nate called me at the Record Store. He needed a good question, something really hard to answer. "Del Ray," he would say. "Give me a tough one. Give me something they'll never get right!"

One of the first trivia questions I came up with was: who was the first black NBA player, what team did he play for, and what University did he come from? A lot of people knew that the first black NBA player was Earl Lloyd. Only a few knew that he played for the Washington Capitols, because the team went out of business after only one season. But nobody remembered that he graduated from West Virginia State, since it wasn't one of the big colleges that was always in the playoffs.

Another question was: who has the winningest goal tender in the NHL? It was Terry Sawchuck, who played for the Red Wings most of his career. One question that I thought might be too easy was: name the production line on the Red Wings. It was Gordie Howe, Sid Abel and Alex Devecchio.

Napoleon ran the trivia sports for a long time. He would call me from the hotel and say, "I need a new question! Make it a hard one. Make it a safe bet for me!"

I would say, "Okay, give me a few minutes, I'll call you back." Then I would think about sports people that I read about, or I'd remember something a sports announcer said during a game. I didn't have any books or encyclopedia to look something up, I just remembered what I'd seen or read. Sooner or later, I'd come up with a question.

Nobody ever got the answer right. At least, not all three parts. Nate didn't offer the game every night, or even every weekend, he mainly added it when things were quiet and he needed to get the audience excited.

His boss finally found out. He wasn't upset, he just told Nate, "Be sure nobody wins, or the weekend comes out of your pay."

In the nine years that Nate ran the sports trivia game, nobody ever got all three questions right. Sometimes they got close, and sometimes they would argue about what was the right answer, but he still never had to pay for somebody to have dinner and stay at the hotel.

My Record and Boutique store was gong good; I was helping my friend Nate with his sports questions, and that was going good. And my dad's party store was providing a good income. The only thing that wasn't going so good was my marriage.

Things were up and down, hot and cold between Yvonne and me. We had put our money down on a nice little tri-level in Southfield. We used most of the money from the Soul Expression lawsuit. I hoped that by us putting all our energy into making a nice home for our daughters, the problems with the marriage would gradually take care of themselves.

I knew something about running a business. And I knew a lot about getting through hard times, surviving injuries and the death of a beloved brother. I guess I didn't know enough about how to make a marriage survive.

CHAPTER TWENTY-SEVEN

Some months after we expanded the store, I got the settlement with the Detroit Police Department. That suit was about the suffering I experienced when the two cops left me to freeze to death in Napoleon's car right before Christmas.

My share of the settlement came to $23,000. Yvonne and I talked about what to do with the money. We decided to buy a house. When Yvonne and I were first married we were kids dreaming of owning a home someday. Now here I was, coming up on my thirtieth birthday, Yvonne was twenty-seven, and we were finally getting the house. It didn't come to us the way we imagined. Our lives didn't turn out anything like we thought they would, but at least we were together. We had that to be thankful for.

We bought a pretty tri-level house in Southfield, a suburb on the West side of Detroit. I especially liked the big yards that all the houses had. They gave a feeling of privacy that you didn't have in our flat in Detroit. Given my disfigurement, I wanted a little distance between me and the neighbors. I didn't want to feel like someone was always watching me.

Yvonne and the girls and I went and picked out furniture for the house. We moved into our very first home in 1978.

Monique was ten and Kim was nine years old, and for the first time in their lives they each had their own bedroom. They seemed very happy in the house. Without hesitating they explored the new neighborhood, with their mother sticking close to them the whole time.

At that time the residents on our block were mostly white. We were the fourth black family in the neighborhood. The other black families included Ray Jarvis, a wide receiver for the Detroit Lions football team, and L.J. Reynolds, a singer with the Dramatics.

I was comfortable living in a white neighborhood. My mom and dad always taught us that people are the same before the eyes of God, and we tried to see our neighbors with the same eyes. The neighbors all seemed to accept us without any prejudice. If they did have any feelings about the change in the neighborhood, we never got a sense of it. Never saw a second glance or heard a mumbled word.

As for my scars and my disabilities, people in Southfield all seemed to accept me exactly as I was. I didn't get any funny looks or find people closing their door when I came by. They accepted me, they were gracious and kind, and the girls and Yvonne made friends just like they did in Detroit.

Things even looked like they were getting better between me and Yvonne. We had the house to organize and make our own. We thought that, if the house was together, our relationship would be together, too. And we were busy helping our daughters adjust to their new school and doing their homework.

We lived in the new house for four years, trying to make our marriage work. Even though there was sometimes a strain between us, I was happy more than words can say. I was living with my daughters just like a real daddy. I could lie on the floor in my own house and play with them. We could all pile up together on the couch and watch TV. We watched all the sports teams, whatever the season. We followed the Red Wings and the Pistons in the winter, the Tigers in the Spring and Summer, and the Lions in the fall.

We watched the regular shows together on television, too. I could laugh with the girls at the funny parts and hide my head with them from the scary parts. I didn't have to worry that it would soon be time for June or Nate to pick me up and take me away from them. Instead I could welcome my friends to our new home and invite them to stay with us.

I always loved helping the girls with their schooling when they were little. Now that we finally had the money to buy the house, we picked a neighborhood that had good schools because Yvonne and I knew how important education was for our daughters' future.

I had been a good student in high school, so it was easy explaining the English and the spelling to the girls. I made up index cards with spelling words on them. I would give them five words at a time. When they learned to spell the five words, I would give them five more. I helped with their math, too. They would compete to see who would finish the fastest.

Yvonne hung a volley ball net in the back yard. I'd watch the girls play for hours. I couldn't play, but I could cheer them on, and that was almost as good. We often had family and friends over for a backyard barbeque. Everybody would get into the volley ball game at some time or another. The girls had nothing but fun. Compared to Detroit our house felt like we were living in a park.

I got them a dog, a big old brown and white St. Bernard we called Bosco. They loved playing with that dog. He was big and clumsy, and he knocked over things when he was in the house. When

Yvonne saw him turn over a table, she said, "That dog's living out-side!" She was right. Bosco was not only clumsy, he slobbered all the time. He left big globs of spit all over the place. We got him a dog house. He lived in that house in the warm weather, and stayed in the garage when it was cold.

The house had a big closet in one of the bedrooms. The girls took it as their playhouse. We left the closet empty so they could make it their little house. They loved to crowd into it with their dolls and make their own private world. We could hear them giggling and shussing each other.

Those were the moments that drew Yvonne and me the clos-est. When our daughters were playing together and giggling, we knew that we were doing something right. We both cherished those times, even though our relationship was often strained.

There was a little park a mile or two from the house. Yvonne and I used to take the girls and Bosco there to play. We would load everything into the car, and Yvonne would drive us over. I still couldn't walk too far, there were calluses on the heels of my feet from the intra-venous catheters. Because of the calluses, I could only walk a short distance. If I was going farther, I used the wheelchair.

We brought hamburgers and hot dogs to the park and cooked them on a charcoal grill. I was pretty good flipping the burgers and the hot dogs with a long fork, although I needed help getting them be-tween the buns. But we all worked together, and the girls took it for granted that there were things I could do and things I could not.

I had missed almost three years with my daughters while I was in the hospital. I missed a lot when I was living at home with my parents, too. Being with the girls every day was like a new world for me, fresh and exciting.

Sometimes, as I watched them play in the park or in the back yard, I would turn my face up to heaven and cry, I was so grateful to have lived to see my girls healthy and happy and at play. When I had been in the hospital I never really believed that I would see this day.

I thanked God every day for this blessing and good fortune. I felt that, whatever happened to me in the future, whatever illness or trouble might come to me, I would be able to accept it, because I had lived to see my daughters start off their lives in a nice home, with a good school and their loving mother watching over them.

Even though we tried to become a real family, Yvonne and I could not overcome the distance between us. We had different experiences. Different ideas about how to be a family. Coming so close to dying like I did, I was grateful to have my family and to watch the children grow. I wanted to do more with them, more for them, but I couldn't, and I had to accept my limits.

Yvonne lost a lot, too. She didn't have the hard-working husband she married. Instead, she was stuck with an invalid who needed more care than the kids. I was afraid that she resented being stuck with a disfigured, helpless man for a husband. Instead of telling her what I was most afraid of, I would get angry with her. That was how I expressed myself, by getting into an argument. As a result, I didn't make her feel much like she was loved or appreciated. But I didn't understand any of that at the time, I was too confused and torn up.

There were two issues that really divided Yvonne and me. The first was the way that I always took care of my friends. Yvonne felt that I let people take advantage of me. It was true, even when we were first married, even before the fire, I always offered to help people. When my friend Pug lost his apartment I invited him and his girlfriend and their child to live with us. I told him it was okay without talking to Yvonne first.

We had a little apartment in Detroit at the time. It was just big enough for Yvonne and me and our two baby daughters. Adding a whole other family really crowded us. The babies crying and waking up at different times didn't help, either.

After two weeks of our living together, I came home to find Pug and his family gone.

"I turned them out," Yvonne said. "You have to take care of your family first."

I was angry about what she'd done; I felt that I was disloyal to a friend. My whole life I had trouble saying no to friends, even if saying yes put a strain on Yvonne.

When our family was together again in the apartment on Strapmore, and now, in the Southfield house, I still had a habit of putting my friends first. I gave away my best suit and pair of shoes. I let people stay with us without first checking it out with my wife.

"You're always taking in bums," she said. I looked on my friends as being less fortunate. Yvonne saw them as mooching off a soft heart.

Part of the difference between me and Yvonne was that my

family had a tradition of taking in needy relations and friends. It went back to my parents' roots in the south, where, poor as you were, there was always a relation or a neighbor down the road who needed your help. You gave them a roof over their head and a bite to eat, even if it meant you went without.

Maybe in helping my friends too much I was looking for praise that I felt I wasn't getting at home. But that wasn't all of it. In our family we always took in people who were down on their luck. It came natural to me.

But Yvonne's roots were in the north, and she wasn't so willing to sacrifice, especially when it took away from her own children. Especially when she had to put up with my friends living with us.

The other issue was my friend, Nate. We spent a lot of time together, even when I was back with Yvonne. Nate always had a girl with him, and she wasn't always the same one. Yvonne worried that, if Nate was fooling around, then I must be doing the same thing. It wasn't true. Nate being my best friend didn't mean that I had to follow his style of life. I just liked hanging out with him.

Even though I was cherishing the time with my daughters, things got more and more tense between Yvonne and me. She wanted to go out with her girlfriends in the evening and have a good time. When we first got married Yvonne was in charge of raising our daughters. I was holding down two jobs, so I spent most of my time at home sleeping.

Besides the fact of my working so many hours, Yvonne had more experience with babies than I did. Growing up, she had a brother who was ten years younger than her, which gave her experience caring for a baby that I never had.

One time when she was pregnant with Kim, she left me with Monique to go shopping. While she was gone I had to change the baby's diapers. I was afraid I would stick her with the safety pin, so I tied the diaper together.

When she came home Yvonne saw the knots on the diaper. She asked me what was going on. I told her, "I ain't sticking my baby with no pins." It was clear that Yvonne would handle the children. That was her role, and she was happy to do it full time.

But now she wanted to do more than raise our daughters and keep the house together. She wanted to go out in the evenings and have fun, while I only wanted to be home with my family. I still wasn't comfortable being out in public.

She was still a caring mother, she just wanted more out of life. I couldn't deal with that. My home was my island; my safe place. I knew she had a right to get out of the house, but at the same time I was terrified that she might find somebody else and fall in love with a real man. That was my biggest fear.

When we were young she had a dream of going to college one day to study business administration, and I had my dream of playing for the Detroit Tigers. It seemed like the fire burned up her dreams as well as mine. I don't know if she resented the fact that my injury took away her dreams, I only knew she was angry with me, and I was just as mad at her.

I began to think that our moving in together was a mistake. Yvonne had built a new life as a single mother without me. Maybe I shouldn't have forced her to give up that life in order to take care of me. I wanted her to be happy, and it got clearer and clearer that she would be miserable as long as she stayed with me.

At the same time, I knew a girl, Pat. When I was in the hospital, she came to see me every day. All the time I was getting operations and therapy, she didn't mind the bandages and my helplessness. She was comfortable with me as I was. She never knew the Delbert McCoy who worked double shifts at the auto plant and played baseball in the snow. She only knew the man who was burned and who sometimes was sunk in despair, but most of the time was hopeful about the future.

Maybe I should have asked Pat to live with me. Maybe I shouldn't have tried to force my marriage to work when it was doomed by the fire. It looked to me like the fire burned up my marriage along with the Soul Expression. Yvonne carried a lot of scars, too; it was just that hers were the kind that didn't show.

I kept on working in the music store. Usually Yvonne or Napoleon would drop me at work, and one of my brothers would get me home. A new, bigger music store opened in the neighborhood. That cut down on sales in my store. Eventually, I had to close the store. I sold the stock to pay the bills, and I ended up without any money from the business.

My hopes for having a business that would carry our family and pay for college for the girls was gone. It was another loss . . .another step backward.

Delbert McCoy

The failure of the store only made things worse at home. We argued over everything. We couldn't get past the anger. Part of me understood that she wasn't the kind of person who was meant to be stuck with me, but I still tried to make her be somebody she wasn't.

A lot of the time I was alone in the house. Yvonne would go out with the girls and not come home. I had to fend for myself. Those were scary days for me, but they turned out to be good ones, too.

One positive result of being left alone was that it forced me to do more for myself. I learned for the first time how to cook a meal. It was mighty tough. I had to try to open a can, but I had only partial use of my right hand—just the thumb and one finger giving me that "pinch" Dr. Herbertson created. My left hand didn't open at all. I couldn't do anything with that. I would hold the can against my chest with my left arm and get the can opener attached with my hand, then I would open the can and make myself some soup. I'd heat it up on the stove right in the can. It wasn't like my mother's cooking, but I got enough to eat.

I got good at feeding myself, too. I learned to hold a spoon in my right hand and keep dipping into the can until I finished the whole thing.

I even got pretty good at doing the dishes. We had a dishwasher, so I'd load up the dirty dishes, and when the machine was full, I'd put in some soap and let her rip.

Dressing myself was very hard. It was my biggest challenge. When your limbs don't bend it's hard to get your trousers over your feet, let alone up your legs and fastened around your waist. I'd lay out my trousers on the floor, stick my feet into them, and raise my legs straight up in the air. When the pants fell down my legs to my hips, I'd lay down my legs, lift my hips, and pull the pants up to my waist.

Mostly, I wore gym shoes. I had them loose enough so I could slip my feet into them, but not so loose that they would fall off when I walked. I slept with my socks on – it was way too difficult for me to pull my socks on and off. For a shirt, I'd usually wear a t shirt and a sweat shirt over it.

But the most important lesson was, I learned to take care of myself.

After a day or two alone in the house, I would have to call Nate, and he would come over and help me. I usually didn't call my brothers or my mom or dad; I didn't want to burden them with my troubles. All through the rocky years living with Yvonne I never told them when things were tense. My parents never told us if they were having problems, and I just naturally did the same.

When Yvonne came back to the house with the girls we'd start to arguing all over again. We argued over everything: money, the girls, my folks, her family. Everything was a battle between us.

The girls would wake up in the middle of the night from me and Yvonne yelling at each other. They would come downstairs to where we were and ask us why we had to fight, why couldn't we get along?

I had no answer for them. I didn't understand what was happening. I was terrified of losing my wife, and I acted on that fear by getting angry at her. Instead of telling her about my fears, I accused her of running out on me.

Yvonne wanted to go out to clubs and dance and have a good time, and I couldn't do that anymore. She was young and pretty. There were men who wanted to take her out. I was filled with anger and jealousy because those guys could dance and drive around in a big car and be carefree, while I had to sit at home in front of the TV and struggle over something as simple as opening a can of soup.

Eventually Yvonne told me she wanted a divorce. I wanted us to stay together. I felt like we could work things out. Was it fair for me to ask her to stay stuck at home with an invalid? No, it wasn't fair, it was selfish, but I asked her to stay with me, anyway.

I believed in my heart that if she had been the one who was hurt and needed a lot of help, then I would have stayed with her and cared for her and done whatever it took. That was who *I* was; it wasn't who *she* was. She was different.

It would have been good if we came to an understanding that we could both live with, but we were too angry and too young to really listen to each other and to work out our differences. We finally decided the best thing to do was to get a divorce and get on with our lives. I gave the house to Yvonne so that she would have a home to raise Monique and Kim. She took over the mortgage.

I moved back in with my parents. I didn't talk to them about what happened, I kept it to myself. I still sent Yvonne money. I wanted to support my children, and I helped with the mortgage as much as I could.

The divorce went pretty smoothly. But there was still a lot of anger between us. I was very angry that she left me and took the children with her. I would have liked it if we could have been neighbors and I could have stayed close to my daughters, but the house in

Delbert McCoy

Southfield was miles from my parent's home in Oak Park.

I was going back to being a part-time father. It didn't seem fair to me; it made me angry and depressed, and I was too immature to understand that a lot of the problem was with me.

CHAPTER TWENTY-EIGHT

My Uncle Pearlie McCoy, who we called Uncle Treetop, was always a happy-go-lucky kind of guy. He was always more concerned with somebody else's problems than he was with his own. My dad gave him the nickname Treetop because, my dad said, "He's always as happy as a bird up in a tree. He acts like he hasn't got a worry in the world. Always whistling and going about his business."

Treetop was married to my mother's sister, Pauline Scott. The two Scott sisters, who were from Maysville, North Carolina, married the McCoy brothers, from Silverdale. My dad, Albert, Sr., met Essie in High School. They married and moved up north. After they came north Pearlie met his sister-in-law's sister, Pauline. He fell in love with her, and they married, too.

Aunt Pauline was a sweet, generous woman, just like her husband. She and Uncle Treetop were the kind of people you could always turn to when you were in trouble. Sometimes one of us kids would be on punishment. We'd visit with Pauline and Treetop, and you could always talk to them; they listened and didn't make judgements.

When I was burned Uncle Treetop was there for me, too. He and my dad helped take me to the tank for the salt water bath. On the weekends when the hospital was short staffed they even helped change my dressings. There was nothing you couldn't ask Uncle Treetop for; he was always ready to help.

Pearlie was always in very good health. The only problem he suffered from was he had these terrible headaches. He had the headaches his whole life.

He would be visiting our house, and we'd see him walking the floor with an ice pack on his head. We knew he was suffering from those headaches. He couldn't sit still, the pain was so bad. But when he wasn't suffering, he was always cracking jokes and making you laugh.

He was tall and thin, like my dad. He was kind of slew-footed, his feet turned out when he walked. On the weekend he wore suits. He was a real nice dresser.

His wife Pauline looked a lot like my mom, you could tell they were sisters. My aunt was a little more strict than my mom. Although she never bore any children, they raised their niece, Wanda Morgan.

They took her in as a baby and brought her up as their own daughter. Later on they helped raise my nephew, young Tony, my brother's son. She was a generous and giving soul.

Like my dad, Pearlie was a veteran of the Second World War. He went to the VA hospital to get treatment for his headaches, and they got a little better. He took aspirin sometimes, but mostly he would put a bag of ice to his head and walk and walk until the headache was better.

He worked at the Kelsey-Hayes plant, where they made auto parts. He worked at that plant for thirty years, until he retired in 1977. After he retired he worked in the church. He was always volunteering, helping out the pastor, Reverend Stout. Pearlie would take care of any little odd job or fix-up that the building needed. He organized the program that distributed government surplus food to the poor. He was always helping others who had less than he did.

Besides helping out at the church, Pearlie loved to cook. He was as good a cook as my mother. Maybe better. After he retired he remodeled his kitchen so he could do even more cooking. He would make a big mess in the kitchen, whipping up one of his meals. My aunt Pauline would scold him about all the pots and pans he would leave in the sink, but secretly she was glad, because he prepared such a great meal.

In 1982, Pearlie was making a real feast. It was the Christmas dinner for the whole family. And, as it often went with his cooking, he realized there was one little thing missing that he needed to complete the meal.

But it was Christmas morning, and all the big grocery stores were shut down for the holiday. Pearlie thought that a little Mom & Pop grocery store that he knew about might be open, so he told his wife, Pauline, he was going to the store to get something for the dinner.

Aunt Pauline went back to sleep. A little while later a neighbor a few doors down from them called her on the phone. She told her, "Mrs. McCoy, your husband left the windshield wipers on. You better tell him to go out and shut them off before he runs the battery down."

Pauline called out for Pearlie, but he didn't answer. She got scared. She looked out the window and saw the windshield wipers going. She knew something bad had happened to her husband.

She looked from room to room, but he wasn't in the house. She put on her robe and slippers and went out to the driveway. There was a little misty-type rain falling. Pauline saw the car door was open. Pearlie was slumped over on the seat. She went to touch him, but he didn't move.

She called EMS, and while she was waiting for the ambulance to arrive, she called our house.

My dad answered the phone. When he recognized her voice, he wished Aunt Pauline a Happy Christmas. She told him, "Albert, I'm scared. I think Treetop is dead!"

My dad asked, "What are you talking about? What's going on?"

She explained how Pearlie needed something for the big Christmas dinner he was cooking, and he decided to try and find a store open. She told my dad how she found him slumped over in the front. He wasn't moving. The ambulance was on the way.

The EMS crew came right away, but they didn't find a pulse. They took him to the hospital anyway. The doctors pronounced him "Dead" in the Emergency Room.

My dad and June went to the hospital to see about Treetop's remains. The rest of the family went over to Aunt Pauline's. Nate and some other friends joined us there. Nate and my cousin Diane McCoy took down a picture on the wall of Uncle Treetop. He was thirty-three in the photo. We were the same age. We were stunned by his sudden death; we couldn't believe it. How could somebody so positive and alive pass away like that? And on Christmas morning.

All of the food that he had prepared never got to be a Christmas dinner. Instead, it was given to the mourners who came to his house to pay respects and to remember the man who was always as happy as a bird in a tree.

The Reverend Stout was in Texas on church business when Uncle Treetop died. He dropped everything and flew back to Detroit, because Pearlie was so loved in the church.

It was a blue holiday for all of us. Everybody was torn apart when we got that call. Treetop was the most loved member of the family. Everybody liked him, even my friends Nate and Pug and the rest.

My mother cried and cried; there was no stopping her tears. We tried to cheer her up, we didn't want her to get sick, we could see she still wasn't over Ball's death. We worried that this loss would really drive her down into despair and sickness.

My dad was in shock, too. He looked like he didn't believe what was happening. He was hoping that Treetop was not dead, just unconscious, which was why he rushed over to the hospital. When he returned from the hospital, my dad confirmed what we already knew, that his brother, my Uncle, had passed.

As for me, I talked with my cousins and friends about how much Uncle Treetop had helped all of us. He took us to the racetrack when we were kids, we had a great time hanging out with him. After I was released from the hospital Uncle Treetop got me really interested in the horses. He took me to the track with him. That helped me get over my shyness, just as June and Nate taking me to the clubs did.

If I got depressed Treetop always was able to help me see a positive side of things. His optimism rubbed off. Over the years he pulled me out of my despair time and time again. He was a warm, giving individual.

Treetop's funeral made me think about other people I had lost, like Ball, killed by the kidnappers in '74. Or Rodney Reno, my good friend, who died from pneumonia in 1972. He was only twenty-two years old when he died. I thought of Boomerang, another friend from childhood, who killed himself because he couldn't deal with being paralyzed from the waist down.

I wondered why God spared me and let these good people die. People who were much healthier than I was. Each one of them passed in the blink of an eye. Their deaths were unexpected. In my life, I came close to death, my heart even stopping three times, but somehow, I survived, for what purpose, I couldn't really say.

If God did have a plan for me, I still didn't know what it was. And Uncle Treetop's death made the whole world seem more scary and uncertain than ever.

CHAPTER TWENTY-NINE

After Yvonne and I were divorced I had a lot of anger toward her. For a year I didn't want to talk to her. I didn't even want to talk to my daughters, who were becoming teenagers. They were coming into their own, with their own ideas about things. Maybe I was unfair to let my anger toward their mother spill over into my relation with my daughters, but that's how it was. I let anger and bitterness get the best of me.

It's normal for teenagers to argue with their parents. Yvonne and me were never as strict as my parents were. Monique and Kim were at that stage when they were trying to act like adults but they didn't have the skills and the experience to always make the right decision. I wasn't there for them during that period in their lives; I was too wrapped up in my own troubles.

At the same time I didn't pay as much attention to my mom as I usually did. I took for granted that she would always be there for me. I imagined that she would be forever making coffee in the kitchen and sitting across from me at the table talking and laughing and being my friend.

I took my father for granted, too. I figured I would always have his strength and his conviction. That he would always be there to lift me up, the way he did when I was in the hospital. It was just about impossible for me to imagine life without both of them.

As the months turned into years our family carried on, following the rhythms of our lives, the way we always did. My dad worked long hours at the Party Store, with me helping out behind the counter. My mom cooked and kept the house, making the dinner and making a home for us all. She encouraged me to be in contact with Monique and Kim. She called them and helped me keep in touch, despite the fact that I was angry and resentful.

In time I let my daughters back into my life. I became more involved in what they were doing at high school, even though I didn't see them every day. I kept telling them, "You got to study hard and go to college. You won't have any kind of good life unless you go to college."

They worked hard in school, and they got good grades. I was sure they would get into college and earn their degrees. Around 1985, Yvonne sold the house in Southfield. She and the girls moved back to Detroit, which made it a little easier for me to see them.

We first noticed that mother wasn't well when she came over to my sister Gwen's house. Gwen was married to Tyrone Lee, a really nice guy. They were living just a few blocks away from my folks, with their kids, Tamika and Carolyn.

Mom had dropped a lot of weight. It happened so gradually that we didn't notice the change until it had gone pretty far. She wasn't just thin; she looked weak, too. And she didn't have that positive way about her that we were used to seeing.

I said, "Mama, you're losing a lot of weight. We have to take you to the doctor."

She had developed diabetes some years before. The doctor was checking on her regularly. He told her he liked the weight loss, because it meant she needed less insulin, plus her sugar was under better control.

But the weight loss was too much. I believe she knew deep down that something was wrong, something serious. She kept saying, "I'm all right, I don't want to go to the doctor," but we finally convinced her that she had to go. I think she put off seeing the doctor because she knew that the news would be bad. She went into the hospital and had the x-rays and blood tests. We all waited anxiously for the results.

On June 27, 1988, her 66th birthday, the doctor gave us the report. We were all together in the hospital waiting room. We wanted the doctor to tell us the news first, then we would decide how to tell her. We all knew that she was sick, but we had no idea how serious it was.

He told us flat out that she had terminal cancer and that she was going to die, there was no getting out of it. It was cancer of the pancreas, which is a very fast-growing cancer. There was no cure for it. Treatment might slow the cancer down some, but in a short period of time it would kill her.

We couldn't believe it.

Gwen and Jackie cried and cried. My dad looked like he'd been hit in the head with an ax handle. His face went blank, and he couldn't speak. He was a zombie. The woman he had loved and lived with for over 40 years was being taken away from him, and he was powerless to stop it.

It was worse than when the kidnappers took Ball and Clifford. At least then we had some hope right up to the time the police identified the body. But this time my mother, my dad's wife, was being kidnapped by cancer, and there was no one to pay the ransom to.

We all made a decision not to tell her that she had cancer. She went through too much, with me being burned and Ball being murdered, and Uncle Treetop's dropping dead on Christmas day. Instead, we told her that the doctors believed she had a "tumor" in her breast. We didn't tell her it was fatal. We said that the doctors wanted to give her chemo therapy so that it didn't become malignant and spread.

She rested a little easy when she heard that. I think she maybe even believed it, although you could not tell for sure, she would never burden us with her suffering. That wasn't her way.

We began taking her to the hospital for chemo therapy. Sometimes the therapy made her really sick, and they had to admit her. She was in and out of the hospital several times. Each time she went back in we were afraid she would leave in a coffin.

Someone in the family was always with her, we never let her be by herself. Not for an hour, not for a minute. When my dad was out of the house working one of us stayed with her. Mostly, we were there because she was so weak and needed so much help, but we were also there because we knew we didn't have much more time with her, and we didn't want to waste a single minute.

One day while she was in the hospital, Gwen and I drove over to visit. Gwen saw the daughter of one of mother's hospital roommates in the lobby. Gwen asked the daughter if she wouldn't mind pushing me upstairs in a wheelchair while she parked the car. The young woman was happy to help.

When I got to her room, mama was crying.

"What's wrong?" I asked her.

"Delray, I'm dying," she told me.

"No you're not," I said. "You're going to get better, just like I did."

She told me that her blood sugar dropped down so low that morning that she passed out. They gave her sugar and brought her back, but she knew her time was coming.

I took her hand and looked into her eyes. They weren't the eyes of the strong, patient woman who cooked all those meals, kept our family clothed and fed, and got us all to church every Sunday. She had always been the quiet strength that held our family together. Now I was looking into the eyes of a fragile, frightened woman.

I told her, "Mama, remember what you used to tell me when I

was in the hospital? That I had to be strong and put my faith in the Lord? That's what you have to do now."

I could hardly hold back the tears. My whole body began to shake. I knew the awful truth, but I wanted to protect her from it.

As soon as Gwen came into the room I went outside and down the hall. I cried like a baby; for myself, for my mother's suffering, for Ball and Treetop up in Heaven, who was going to be with my mother again, and for everyone in our family.

The lies that we told her made the whole sickness and dying even harder. It made a wall between us, where we always had been honest and close. But we had decided as a family not to tell her the truth, and nobody wanted to change the plan.

Somehow she got through a last round of chemo-therapy and lived to come home one more time. We decided to throw her a birthday party. Aunt Pauline and Gwen and Jackie cooked. We decorated the basement and invited all of her friends.

Everybody loved my mother. I mean, *everybody*. The kids on the block, their parents, all our in-laws—they all loved her. Even boyfriends and girlfriends who came around when we were young liked my mom. She was just one of those persons who never had a cross word for anyone, only a kind one.

She cooked for anyone and everyone who came into the house. Kids in the neighborhood always knew they could fill their bellies by coming by, and often they didn't have all that much on the table at home.

The day of the party my dad and Tony walked mama down the stairs to the basement. She was too weak to go down by herself. Her face lit up in a big smile when she saw so many people. I don't think I saw her look that happy since the time before Ball died. She ate a little piece of cake, she couldn't hold down much food. Mostly she sat and looked at everybody and smiled.

She didn't last long at the party. My dad and Tony helped her upstairs. She went to bed and fell asleep.

There weren't many gifts we could buy her; what could she enjoy? One thing we did to make mama feel better, besides the big party, was to arrange for her to meet her favorite TV star. That was Nell Carter, who was starring in a show called *Give me A Break*. Mama never missed a single episode, no matter how sick she was.

Nell Carter came to visit her, which was very kind of her, and that made mama as happy as the party we gave her.

We stayed up all night, watching over her twenty-four hours a day. Friends helped us. People she had helped raise who looked on her as their mother. There was always somebody to take her to her chemo therapy treatments at the hospital, to stay with her while she got the treatment, and to bring her home.

She was slipping away from us. Each day she slept a little longer, and drank a little less. She ate no food, she just took liquids. The skin on her face was drawn tight over the bones.

One morning after her chemo, my dad went in to wash her up and maybe lift her into a chair. She was paralyzed and blind. She told him that she lost her sight several days before, but she didn't want to trouble us with the news, she knew it would upset us all.

We brought her back to the hospital. She lasted four days. A massive heart attack ended her suffering. She died on August 19, 1988, just two months after she was diagnosed with the cancer.

We held the funeral at the Oakland Baptist Church. It's the church where our family worshiped when we were children. My brothers and sisters and I had gone to Sunday school there when we were kids. We were in the Boy Scouts and the Girl Scouts, and the choir, too. It was truly like going home, having the service there. Reverend Larry Walker was the minister. He gave a beautiful eulogy.

There's a song by the Spinners that came out around the time that mama was sick. It's called *Sadie*. There's a line that goes, "If there's a Heaven up above, I know you'll be teaching angels how to love." Whenever I hear that song, I think of her.

There could be no replacement for the joy she always brought to us. Like losing my brother and my uncle, losing my mother was a terrible shock to the family. The only comfort that we had was knowing that she was bringing happiness to Ball and Treetop, who were waiting for her in Heaven.

CHAPTER THIRTY

After my mom died I stayed with my dad in the house in Oak Park for several years. We didn't talk much about her passing. Both of us held in our hurt. But I could see how much he missed her. My mom was always the heart of our family. She was the one who organized the holiday get-togethers. Who picked out the presents for us when we were kids. She would always make two pots of coffee in the morning, regular coffee for my dad and anyone else who was visiting, and Sanka for her and me. We would sit around drinking the coffee and talking. She had raised June's son, Maurice, from a baby. She was always there to take care of anybody who needed help.

It seemed like Ball's death in 1974 took a lot of the joy out of our holidays. Uncle Treetop's death made them even sadder and more lonely. But when my mom passed, the holidays weren't just joyless, they were depressing. Dismal. Painful. My sister Gwen tried to take on the job of organizing Thanksgiving and Christmas, but the family never regained the joy we once knew.

One thing that came out of my mother's death was that my daughters developed a real interest in our family's roots. They were in their early twenties, and they wanted to know about our family tree. They wanted to know about their great-grandparents, who had the farms in Maysville and Silverdale. We told them about the farmhouse that had no running water, and how you had to go outside to get water and to use the outhouse.

My dad showed them pictures and told them stories about curing the tobacco in his father's barn. I told them how the pigs scared me when me and my brothers were down in the summer. My daughters really enjoyed learning about the older generations.

My dad and I worked at keeping our family together. Like always, we took in relatives who needed help. Slow's son, young Tony, was living with us. His mom, Anita, and my brother Slow (Tony) argued a lot and they didn't live together. After Uncle Treetop died, young Tony lived with his mom for a while. After my mom passed, he came and lived with me and my dad.

Ball's son, Derron, lived with us, too. He had moved in after Ball's death, in 1974. My sister Jackie's son Frederick moved in around 1981. He needed someone to tutor him with his schooling, he was having trouble with math and science, so he lived with us and I coached him in his studies. In the period after my mother's death, we had four nephews living with my dad and me.

Even before I was burned I never put on much weight. After the fire I stayed the same size as when I was a teenager. Now my nephews and I shared our clothes, just like me and my brothers did when I was growing up.

I helped them with their homework. We talked about girls. They asked me what sort of things I did when I was young, did I ever get in trouble. I told them some of the things I did when I was their age, like the parties at Shorty's basement with the Silver Satin wine mixed with Kool aid. I told them about the gambling at Johnny's, and the time I rescued Nate from Johnny's house by throwing a brick through the front window.

I told them about the time I smoked marijuana, how it made me sick for three days, and I never again took drugs, not even after I was out of the hospital. Even in the times when I was depressed I never buried my despair in drugs. I made that very clear to them.

My nephews didn't get into drinking or drugs, as far as I could tell. They didn't even smoke cigarettes. They were good kids. Their grades were good and they didn't miss a lot of school. I knew they were growing up okay.

I was growing more independent than ever. As a result, my nephews didn't have to do as much for me as my brothers and friends had to when I first came home from the hospital. My nephews pitched in with the chores, and we lived like a pack of bachelors.

My dad sold the Party Store. He was old enough to retire, but he liked to keep busy, just like Uncle Treetop. He was always working. He got a job as a security guard in the local library. He owned an apartment building that June managed, too.

After my daughter Monique graduated from college, she began studying for her law degree at Wayne State University in Detroit. Kim was at the same school studying part-time for her accounting degree. And Yvonne and I were talking. In fact, we were getting along pretty good, even though she never said anything to me about us getting back together. I wanted to hold on to the feeling that we would be together again some day, but at the same time I wanted someone with me who loved me and I loved back.

I put a lot of energy into telling my nephews how important it was for them to study hard, get good grades, and to go to college. I helped my nephews with their homework, just like I did with my daugh-

ters. I kept on telling them, "Study hard. Stay in school. Go to college
. . . *be somebody.*"

Young Tony and Derron started saying, "Why don't you go to
college Uncle Delbert?" Monique and Kim were telling me the same
thing. When my mother was alive, she always said, of the four boys, I
was the one she thought would go to college.

I thought about it for a good long while. I told myself that I
didn't fulfill my mother's wishes while she was alive, but I could fulfill them after her death. I decided to do it.

Liberty University, in Lynchburg, Virginia, had a special correspondence program for handicapped people like me. They sent you
a computer and you studied on it. When it came time to take tests, they
sent a proctor to observe you, and then the test was sent to the school to
be read.

I studied marketing. I knew that the record store failed in part
because we weren't good at getting known to the public. I decided to
get the training I needed so that I could be successful the next time I
started a business.

When my dad and I talked, it was usually about sports. We
often didn't agree on things. He was hard on the Detroit teams. Very
critical. He acted like he was down on them, but I knew that secretly
he was rooting for them.

One thing that my dad and I did together was play the horses.
He loved the racetrack. He was the one who did the actual betting,
while I helped him pick out the horses. In those days we didn't have
off-track betting, and he didn't like to mess around with a bookie. So
he relied on me to handicap the horses.

The horses ran at Hazel Park and Northfield. He would get me
the racetrack book from the park, which had information on the horses.
And he would bring me a couple of newspapers that had racing tips
and ask me to look them over.

I picked the horses by comparing the speed rating, the past
performance, and what class they were in. I also looked hard at what
horse made the most money in his career, not just in the last year. I
compared the horse's past year with his career to see if he was still
strong and a good candidate.

For many years I read the statistics of all the sports teams.
When I was in the hospital with nothing to do, I studied those numbers
hard. When I got out, I recommended sports teams to bet on to Nate,

who passed the tip on to his customers. All those years of studying sports teams made it easy for me to handicap the horses for my dad.

It was Treetop who first taught me about horse racing. He loved to play the horses, too; it went along with his happy-go-lucky nature. He got my dad interested in the sport. That was how my dad got so keen on going to the track.

I usually recommended a horse for the last three races on the program. That way, by the time he got home from work and rested up, my dad could still go out to Hazel Park and place his bets. If he hit, he would give me a share for picking it. But if he lost he was out the money and no hard feelings.

We made some good money for a while. He never bet with a bookie, he was strict about going to the track and placing his bet properly. Today you can bet off-track, the state allows it, but back then the only legal way was at the track.

As much as I enjoyed helping my nephews and my dad, I was too isolated at the house. It was beginning to look like Yvonne and I were going our own way, and that we would never get back together again. I accepted that and decided that I needed to move on to a new relationship.

It looked to me like the only way to get involved and have a relation and meet people was to be in my own place. I wanted to know if I could meet somebody to live with. Start a new relationship with a woman. Maybe even get married again some day.

In 1992 I decided it was time for me to try living on my own. I'd been dependent on people for my day-to-day functions ever since the fire. I'd been through a divorce, I was working on a college degree, and most important of all, I was getting a lot better at taking care of myself. It seemed like it was now or never: time to go out into the world and see if I could be my own man.

My daughters still meant the world to me, and I still cared a lot for Yvonne. It wasn't that I was giving up on them, just that I needed to see if I could make a life for myself.

Moving out of the house didn't mean that I didn't love my dad, either. We weren't arguing or anything like that. We got along like we always did. He was still my dad, which meant that he still needed to try and take care of me. It was only natural for a father to feel that way toward his son. And given that his son was so disabled, it was also natural for him to be protective of me.

Delbert McCoy

He understood that there comes a time for a son to get out from under the protective wing of his father. I had to find out if I could sustain my life on my own, the way I did when I was nineteen and holding down two jobs.

My sister Gwen and her husband, Tyrone Lee, were fixing up a house for a rental property on Turner Avenue in Detroit. Tyrone told me that after they got the new place fixed up, I could move into the house and rent it from them. They didn't charge me hardly any rent. It was a terrific deal. He was a great guy who gave me the opportunity to get out on my own.

The nephews wound up coming with me. Derron was 19, he worked in a factory. Fred was 17, he was in his last year of high school, so he only worked part-time after school. Tony was 18, and he had a job, too. I was getting a monthly check from social security, so putting it all together, we were able to pay our way.

I had my own room for the first time in my whole life. That was a great experience. I'd never been really on my own before, I always had family around me. Now I wasn't living with a parent or a wife, just the nephews, who looked to me for guidance. I was the grownup in charge of the house.

The only furniture we had in the beginning was a big screen TV that I brought with me. I got a Montgomery Ward living room set, and got some used furniture, too. The nephews helped out, they saved. Soon we got a couch to go with the TV.

My dad gave me one of the bedroom sets from the house. We got an icebox and a stove, and we were in business.

We all pitched in and worked together. Gwen and Tyrone continued to give us a break on the rent, so it didn't cost us too much. The nephews paid the utilities and a little something for the rent, and we had food on the table, even if we didn't have much in the way of furniture.

We divided up the chores four ways. Everybody did their part. One of the guys did the cooking, another did the cleaning, and another did the laundry. I kept the bills, adding everything up and sending out the checks every month. We were organized, and we ate pretty good for a bunch of bachelors.

In June, 1992, my father had a big family reunion in the back yard of his house in Oak Park. People came from all over the country – from Pennsylvania, North Carolina, from New York and New Jersey –

171

it was a great get together. We didn't fill Tiger Stadium, but we had over a hundred people spilling out of the yard.

My dad and his brother Pearlie, who died in 1982, married two sisters, Essie Mae (my mother) and Pauline. At this family reunion we naturally had people from both sides of the family come.

Aunt Pauline and Gwen and Jackie did most of the cooking. They used a lot of Uncle Pearlie's best recipes, especially his barbecue sauce, which was famous in the family. Even though he wasn't with us, his spirit was there in the food that we ate.

There were cousins at the party I hadn't seen for years. Ronnie, one of the cousins, lives in Detroit. He used to go down to Silverdale with us when we were kids and work on Grandfather McCoy's farm. We talked about those summers, laughing and telling stories about the mules and the tobacco that cured in the barn, with the hot oven in the middle of the summer.

We played a lot of the old Motown songs, too. Nate and I had gone and bought some CD collections of the old songs. When we played James Brown, my cousin Ronnie did the James Brown moves, just to show us that he still had it. We applauded and cheered him, just like when we were kids.

A nephew of mine, Maurice, brought a friend of his, a woman named Renee. He introduced me to her, and we soon got to talking. We talked about our family – she had four children – and I told her about my daughters, who were young women now, they weren't children. I pointed them out to her, and she met them, too.

She fed me cake that day. I could do it myself, but she wanted to be nice to me, so I let her help. We talked some more. Pretty soon we were laughing and sharing experiences as if we'd known each other for years, not just for an hour or two. I introduced her to Yvonne and to other relatives who came by the table.

We just talked and kept on talking. When the party started to end, I asked Renee, was she going steady with anybody? She told me no, she wasn't. She asked, was I going with anybody? I told her, No, I was staying on Turner with my friend Napoleon and my nephews. I gave her my phone number, she gave me hers. I left the party feeling on top of the world. I met a woman who liked me just the way I was, and I couldn't wait to see her again.

I was surprised at how quickly I asked her for her number. When I was young, I was always shy around girls. You would think that, with my face being burned and all of my disabilities, I would be even more shy around a woman. After all, there were plenty of good-looking men at the party who could dance with her, or drive her around in their car, or take her to a club.

In Saint Joseph Mercy Hospital, when they were giving me physical therapy, the nurses like Miss Haab helped me get over my shyness. They forced me to sit out in the hall where people could see me, and they made me walk all the way down the hall to the lounge and back.

After a while, I got over some of my fears about being seen in public. I even started to joke about my injuries. One time, when a nurse asked how come I didn't get burned in my genitals, I told her I urinated on myself to put the fire out. I told that joke a lot after that. I learned to see the humorous side of my situation. Over the years in the hospital I got over a lot of my shyness.

When I got out of the hospital, I still had a lot of fear that Yvonne would think that I was ugly because of my scars. I was afraid that she wouldn't want to be around me. Nate used to tell me, "Women don't look at your face, they look into your heart." He was one of the most important persons to help me get over my fears with women. He would always tell me, "They don't see the scars, they look inside you. That's what love is about."

When I first got out of the hospital and was living at home, Nate and Luther and Lamont all got me to go out with them to a club. I didn't want to go at first, but they would drag me with them. I would sit at a table and have a beer and talk, and nobody really paid any attention to the way I looked. They mostly took me the way I was.

Working at the Party and the Record Store helped me get over my shyness too, because I was forced to be out in public. Uncle Tree-top taking me to the racetrack helped too. It was a good feeling being in a crowd that was cheering and focusing on the event, and not paying any attention to me at all.

By the time of the family reunion, I had a lot more confidence in myself, because I knew that I was a decent person. It felt good to know that there was a woman who liked me the way I was.

After the family reunion, Renee and I started talking on the phone. Then she started coming over to the house. We got closer and closer. It seemed like there was a natural love growing between us.

CHAPTER THIRTY-ONE

A couple of months after my nephews and me moved into the house on Turner, Napoleon moved in with us. While he was with us, Nate suggested that we try and get a catering business together. I was working on my degree in marketing from Liberty University, the correspondence course was going along good, and I was dreaming of starting up another business. Napoleon had a lot of experience in the food and entertainment industry, so he took charge of that part. Plus, Nate knew a lot of people he thought would use the service.

We saved up a little money, we bought some tables and chairs, a cake stand, and all the things we needed to cook. He got his sisters to cook for us. We made enough money to be able to pay some rent. The business was up and down for a couple of years. We struggled to get customers. It was tough, because we didn't have a storefront to really sell our product. By working out of our house, we couldn't put up a really professional image for the customer to see. But we kept at it.

I used the marketing techniques I was learning from school to promote the business. I made out flyers and passed them around at malls, churches, and throughout the neighborhood. The events we catered got us a good word of mouth, which brought in more customers from around the area.

In 1994 we catered a big graduation party for me and Monique. Monique had finished her law degree, and I had got my marketing degree. We used the occasion to show off the catering business, as well as to celebrate our success.

The party was in my dad's backyard, just like the family reunion of two years ago. This time, we got the yard looking like a disco. We had two tents, a band, tables and chairs, and a concrete area we used for dancing. We invited *everybody,* and over 200 people came.

The candles and napkins and tablecloths were designed by Nate and Rene. They used the colors of Wayne State, Monique's school, blue and red, and my school, Lynchburg University, which were white and gold. The whole setting was beautiful to behold.

The party got us a little business, but we were handicapped by working out of our home. We were in the situation where we had to expand, buy a store, and operate a retail side along with the catering. But I'd had enough of the retail business, working all those years in the record store. Besides, we didn't have any way to raise the capital we

174

would need. After a while, business started slacking off.

Nate was working as a manager at a club on Van Dyke, so he couldn't dedicate the time we needed to make it take off.

The Tigers weren't having a good year, either. They were a long way from the World Series winners of 1968 and 1984. But Sparky Anderson was managing some great players, Alan Trammel, Lou Whitaker, Jack Morris and Kirk Gibson, and I kept hoping they would make it back to the World Series.

Even if my Tigers weren't going to win a World Series, I was on a real winning streak. Renee and I were getting along so good, we decided to move in together. The house where I was living with my nephews and Nate had a finished basement. Derron, Frederick and Tony moved downstairs and had their own apartment. Renee and I shared my bedroom. Nate still had his own room, and Renee's kids - Spike, Bill, Marcus and Nicole - got the third bedroom. We didn't have to pack her kids two to a bed, the way I slept when I was growing up. Instead, we got them bunk beds, so everybody had their own bed.

I still saw my daughters a lot. In fact, I saw a lot of Yvonne, too. She and Renee got along good. That made me really happy. I had Renee with me, my daughters were in college and doing well, and I was growing more confident and independent. My dad even had a new girlfriend.

Love was definitely in the air. It seemed like my life was coming together. I was optimistic about the future, a little bit like when I was young before the fire.

One evening, me and Renee really had a good laugh. Nate and I were over at Renee's grandmother's house. We were sitting around having dinner. Nate looked hard at Renee's grandmother; her name is Essie, just like my mother. He said, "You look familiar to me. I know I know you from somewhere."

We talked about it. Finally, it came out. Essie had worked at the Ponchetrain hotel in the nineteen sixties. She worked in the kitchen. Nate and I both had part-time jobs as busboys at the hotel. As soon as we made the connection, I remembered her, too.

Then, to really make us all laugh, Nate remembered a day when Essie brought her two granddaughters to work. They were little girls, just two or three years old. One of them was Renee! So it turned out that I met Renee when she was a little girl. It was almost like we were destined to meet, we just had to wait a little over twenty-five years for destiny to really bring us together.

CHAPTER THIRTY-TWO

Renee and I were doing pretty good, living in Detroit on Turner off Six Mile Road, with her children. Renee's sons, Bill and Charles, who we call Spike, were playing basketball at Fitzgerald Post middle school. Bill was pretty good, he played guard; Spike played forward. They were selling M&M's to raise money for the team equipment. Uniforms and stuff like that. Two of Rene's sons were with me. Bill was really working hard at his game. Every time you saw him he had a basketball in his hand. We used to tell him he wanted to be like Michael Jordan, and we thought he could do it. Spike was a good rebounder; he was a Dennis Rodman type. He was more physical, he didn't mind taking an elbow, and like Rodman, he could give it as well as take it.

I didn't want to poach on their territory, that wouldn't be fair to the team. So Renee dropped them at one mall, and then she took me to another down the road.

Bill had to sell M&M's for his school to raise money for the basketball team. Rene said to me, "Delbert, I bet you could make some money selling candy, too."

After thinking about it for a little while I decided to give it a try. I liked talking to people. This would give me a chance to meet them. More important, it would help pay for plastic surgery. Medicare called plastic surgery cosmetic. They wouldn't cover it. I hoped to earn enough to cover the costs of several operations; there was still a lot of work to do to make me well.

I started my first day selling candy at the Oak Park Fruit Market. It was in a large mall in Oak Park on Nine Mile and Coolidge. Renee took me and Bill and dropped us off. Bill helped pull my wheelchair out of the car, and I spent my day in it. My legs weren't strong enough for me to stand for hours at a time.

There were several big stores at the mall. We each took a different store so we wouldn't compete with one another. The sales went pretty good. I didn't think it was right for me to ask people to buy from me. I just held out my box of candy, and if somebody wanted to buy, I would tell them how much it cost.

At first I was nervous because I didn't know how people would treat me; if they would look at me funny, or even say something insulting. But they didn't. Everyone treated me with respect. If they didn't want to buy the candy they would still wish me a nice day or wish me well.

I guess I could have been more aggressive. But it didn't feel right to me to come out with a story and a lot of talk. That was too much like the winos who panhandle for change. I wasn't in their shoes, I was a survivor. I didn't drink or take drugs, and I didn't want anyone thinking that I was down and out or addicted.

After that first day selling candy we started going to a different mall every weekend. I sold candy in malls in Rochester, West Bloomfield, Brighton—all of the towns around Detroit. I never made a lot of money, but it got me out of the house and got me meeting people.

Sometimes Bill's brothers came along to raise money for their school. Each of us would pick a different store. After a while, people got to know me. I became a regular outside the fruit and vegetable market on Coolidge. People who saw me a couple of times got to stopping and talking. They would ask how I got burned. I would tell them a little bit about the fire at the Soul Expression. After they heard my story they would tell me one of their own. I was surprised at how many tragedies had fallen to people. Very few of them had scars like me, but once you got to know them, you learned they had experienced great suffering in their lives.

For some reason which I didn't understand, many of the people who told me their story ended by saying that they felt better by sharing it with me. Quite a few said things like, "My life can't be half as bad as I thought, hearing what you've been through."

A lot of the time they would say they were inspired by my willingness to sit in the mall and try to help myself. I didn't see my selling candy as particularly brave. I just saw it as a chance to get out and meet people and to try and help myself and family.

A few people did have the wrong idea when they first saw me. They figured I was a drug addict. One woman asked me if I was burned from drugs. She was confusing me with Richard Pryor, who was burned when he was freebasing cocaine. I told her I was burned in a fire at a club in downtown Detroit. She went away without buying any candy.

But most people didn't assume from looking at me that I was a drug addict or an alcoholic or a homeless person. They accepted me as somebody who was trying to help himself out, and they bought my candy without any problems.

Often I ran into people who knew me back when I was at Detroit General Hospital. One day a short, nice looking middle-aged woman came up to me where I was selling candy. She asked, "Are you Delbert?"

I told her I was. I knew her face, even though I couldn't say where I met her. But that smile, it was so familiar, I said to myself, "This has to be Marlene."

Then she said, "It's me, Marlene. I was your nurse at Detroit General. Remember?"

She was married, had children, and was living in the suburbs. She was so glad to see me, she came up and gave me a hug. We talked about those days in the hospital. I didn't know it at the time, but she and a lot of the other nurses in the Intensive Care Unit were new graduates who were put into the ICU because of the nursing shortage.

"I was almost as scared as you were," she told me with a smile.

"You hid it pretty good, I never knew," I said.

We parted with her promising to see me again. I knew I would, she lived in Rochester Hills, which was not far away.

The day I met the fireman, that was really surprising. One afternoon, a man came up to me. He had gray hair. He was ver polite. He said, "Excuse me, do you mind if I ask you how you got burned?"

I told him that I was burned in a fire at the Soul Expression back in 1969. The man told me that he was a Detroit fireman, and he had fought that very fire. He remembered it well.

"It was a bad fire," he said. "It was very hot. We were able to extinguish it quickly, but by the time we got there the building was mostly destroyed. The chemicals in the Dry Cleaning store made a mess of it."

The fireman, who was now retired, wished me well and went on. A few days after that I met a man who drove one of the ambulances that carried victims from the Soul Expression to Henry Ford hospital. He didn't carry *me*, but he remembered the burn victim he transported well. She was a young girl who had burns on her arms and hands. He said that the scene outside the club had been wild. Pandemonium. It was one of the worst evacuations he ever saw.

I also met Sharon Klein, the social worker who was on duty the night that I was brought to the Emergency Room. Between reuniting with old friends and making new ones, my days at the malls became a happy experience.

In 1997 the Detroit News ran a wonderful article about me, written by Kate Lawson. It told my whole story, from when I was burned to my treatment at Detroit General and St. Joseph Mercy Hospital. Kate wrote a very sympathetic article with a lot of pictures. The article showed the public that I wasn't a drug addict or a panhandler. After that, even more people started coming up to me and telling me their stories.

I learned a lot from Kate Lawson's article, too. She had done a good deal of research into my story. I learned that the two men who set the fire, Eugene Kelley and Ron Robinson, were no longer in jail. They appealed their life sentence to the Michigan Supreme Court. The Supreme Court overturned their conviction. They ruled that gasoline poured on a building wasn't an explosive. As a result, they only served the eight year sentence for setting the fire and malicious destruction of property.

My dad and I were surprised to hear the arsonists were out. It seemed there was no justice in it. Everyone was amazed that the judge would rule like that. But there was nothing we could do about it. All we could do was keep on going and put it behind us.

One special person who read the Kate Lawson article was Dr. Sandra Brown. Dr. Brown is a skin specialist. She's a pioneer in treating African-Americans who have been burned or suffered other injuries to their skin. After reading the article Dr. Brown called Kate Lawson at the Detroit News, and Kate called me. After that, Dr. Brown began doing treatments on my face. The treatments allowed me to close my eyes completely for the first time since the fire. I finally would be free from the eye infections that plagued me for years.

Her treatments released scar tissue that had made my face real tight for many years. I felt relief from the tightness in the skin around my eyes and mouth. That made my much more comfortable. I could smile more easily, and smiling is the best face you can show people. Especially to friends.

I went once a week for the treatments. One day we got to talking. I started telling Dr. Brown about my old school, McMichael Junior High School.

"Wait a minute," she said, "I went to that school, too."

One thing led to another. I talked about a shop class I had with Mr. Longnecker. Dr. Brown asked me, "Were you in the class when a guy was throwing a hat around the room? It ended on a girl's desk. The guy who lost his hat came up and hit the girl."

She was the girl who got hit. I remembered that day well. It turned out we were classmates. I told her the name of the guy. We got a big laugh over it. The more we talked, the more we found we had in common. It seemed like destiny meant for us to meet again, just like it meant for me and Renee to hook up years after that visit at the hotel Ponchetrain.

I also went to a Plastic Surgeon at the University Hospital in Ann Arbor. Dr. Garner worked on my eyes and nose. After that, I met a woman in Troy, on Maple and Coolidge, at the Whole Foods Store. She told me about a Dr. Jackson, a plastic surgeon, who operated on her daughter. "He's very good," she said, "and very understanding."

She set up an appointment with Dr. Jackson. He operated on my upper lip. He also put expansion tubes on the sides of my head under the skin. The expansion tubes were to construct a new pair of ears; mine were completely burned off in the fire. Now that I was older I needed ears to hang a pair of glasses on. Of course, I also wanted to look more normal, and a man without ears looks very strange.

There were two DJ's on the radio station 98.7, Coco and Mason, who talked about issues that are important to the community, as well as playing Rap and R&B music. They talked about Kate Lawson's article in the Daily News on their show. After that, even more people came up to me when I sold candy. I met Barry Sanders, the football great, who told me to "keep fighting." And Earl Clue, the jazz musician, who said I was a "great inspiration." Terry Fair, another football player with the Detroit Lions, came up and told me he was glad that I was trying to help myself. He said he liked my courage, and told me to keep fighting.

Mike and Drew, DJ's at radio station WRIF, 101 FM, also took up my case. They talked about me on the radio. When one town forbade me to sell candy at their mall, Mike and Drew sponsored me at different events. They allowed me to sell candy, and they spoke about me on their shows almost every day.

Just this year I met one of my heroes while selling candy in front of the Kroger in Bloomfield on Lasher and Maple Rd. I was sitting in my wheelchair, like I always do. It was around 5 PM, a real nice evening. I was selling Kit Kats and Reese's Pieces, instead of M&M's.

A man in a nice suit came up to me. He told me he was the Press secretary and marketing agent for Gordie Howe. He said that he and Gordie had read the article about me in the Detroit News.

The secretary's name was Del, which is what my dad always

called me. He said that Gordie and his wife Colleen wanted to meet me. He called them on his cell phone.

About 20 minutes later Gordie and Colleen came up to me. Gordie introduced himself, which he didn't have to do, I recognized him right away. He looked like he did when he played hockey, just a little older, with a touch of gray in his hair.

He shook my hand, saying, "I read your article. I like what you're doing. I think you've got a lot of courage."

His wife was a real nice woman with a radiant smile. I could tell right away that she was very compassionate and concerned for people. I knew from the papers that Mr. and Mrs. Howe did a lot of charity work. Their kindness came through the minute they met me.

Gordie autographed my candy box, saying it might boost sales a little. Then he autographed his book, *And…Howe*, and gave it to me.

Renee was just pulling up in the big conversion van when Gordie and his wife came out. She came over, and Del took pictures of me, Gordie, Colleen and Renee.

He talked for a minute about his career. He said that when he scored his 700th goal— it was in Quebec—the applause he got really moved him. "That was a day I'll never forget," he said.

Then Gordie really surprised me. He asked if I would do some speaking engagements with him. "I'm tired of doing all the speaking," he said. "Maybe you could give me some slack and do some of the talking."

Gordie's agent Del said that I might be able to speak at two or three engagements. Gordie said, "Nah, he can do them all. I need the rest."

He said it with a smile, but I knew he meant business. I told him that I would be honored. If there was anything that I could say that would help people deal with their troubles, it was okay by me.

Before he left Gordie turned to me with a twinkle in his eye and said, "By the way, it might help if you knew something about hockey. Do you?"

I chuckled at that, remembering when I was a patient in Rehab at Saint Joseph Mercy Hospital. Some of the nurses were big Red Wings fan, especially one RN and her daughter. They would come into my room whenever there was a game on and ask, "What's the score? Who's winning?" Sometimes they would watch part of the game with me, depending on how busy they were. The nurses there got me hooked on hockey.

I grinned and said to Gordie, "I know a few things."

He said, "Okay, what was the name of the line I played on?"

"It was called 'The Production Line,'" I told him. "The line had you, Alex Divecchio and Sid Abel ."

Then I told him, "I followed your sons, Mark and Marty, when they got into the game. Mark played for the Red Wings at the end of his career. Marty played, too. Was he with Quebec?"

He laughed again. "That's right, Marty played in Quebec. I guess you do know about hockey."

Gordie had a great sense of humor. He and his wife and Del said good-bye, Renee helped me load the wheelchair into the van, and we drove home to tell the kids about who we met at the mall that day.

Through the article in the Detroit News a couple of lawyers called me on the phone. They were Robert Lippett and Roger Meyers. They did some work with Medicare for me, which got the government to help pay for my plastic surgery.

People at General Motors got involved, too. Harry Pierce, their vice-president, and their Medical Directors, Mr. Conlan, and Roderick Gullum, worked with the lawyers to get Medicare to take care of my needs. Medicare agreed to pay for 80% of the surgical work. I raised the rest.

I was finally getting the surgery I needed to complete the rehabilitation of my body; I was meeting old friends and sports heroes. And I was blessed with the love of a wonderful woman. The sun seemed to be shining every day, and in Detroit, that's really something.

CHAPTER THIRTY-THREE

If you grow up in Michigan, you grow up around hunters. When I was working in the auto plants I always knew somebody who went "up north" to hunt. It was a very popular sport. People hunted for deer or black bear, raccoon, possum, pheasant or quail. Ducks were very popular, too.

If you lived on a farm, and especially if you were poor, you ate a lot of wild game that you shot or trapped yourself. We always ate wild meat in my family. We had it on grandfather's farm, and my mom cooked it at home, too. She cooked possum and raccoon and rabbit, just like they did down south. My Uncle Treetop cooked game when he was alive, and my brother June makes stew with deer meat. His dumplings and gravy are the best.

In Detroit, I had a friend, Keith Thomas, who liked to hunt deer. Keith is from Pennsylvania. He moved to Detroit, where he did a lot of mechanical work for my nephews. He's a great man with brakes. He's very good with plumbing and heating systems, too.

His whole family back in Pennsylvania liked to hunt. One time early in December, in 1996, Keith's brother told him he had some deer meat, some rabbit and squirrel, and if Keith drove down from Detroit he could have all he wanted.

Keith asked me if I wanted to ride with him. He had a conversion van that was very comfortable. We could even sleep in it if we got tired and needed to pull over. He offered to let me have all the game I wanted. I told him I'd like to go. We set out on December second, leaving in the evening. We got in to his brother's place around midnight.

After we picked out the meat and had it packed in the van, we slept for four or five hours. We left Pennsylvania around seven in the morning, after Keith caught a few hours sleep.

I was riding shotgun in the passenger seat. Somewhere in Ohio, I fell asleep, with my legs propped up on the dashboard. All of a sudden, I woke up, and I saw Keith standing up and looking down at me. At first, I didn't understand why he wasn't in the driver's seat, driving. Why we weren't moving.

Then I began to feel the pain in my legs, and it suddenly hit me: we were in an accident. I felt like my right leg was crushed. I looked at it, but I didn't see anything lying on it and pressing on it. My other leg was swollen around the lower part really bad. I couldn't move the left one at all.

Pretty soon the ambulance came. Two paramedics, a lady and a guy, looked at me through the window. A state trooper came up, too. They got into the van and told me they had to get me out and take me to the hospital.

I told them, "Please don't move me, I'm in a lot of pain. Please don't move me."

The pain was worse than anything I experienced from the fire. It was worse than being burned on the stairway. It was worse than the dressing changes or the salt water in the tank at Detroit General. It was worse than anything I ever knew.

The trooper told me there was gasoline leaking from the van. "We have to get you out of there, sir. You could be burned to death."

The paramedic explained that they had to get me medical help, too. She put her hand on my forehead and rubbed it, sort of like the way Dr. Grifka used to touch me forehead. "We have to move you, hon," she said gently. "We just have to."

They put a neck brace on me, then they brought in a long board and placed it next to me. They started to roll me over, and I hollered bloody murder. The pain was terrible. They slid me onto the board and strapped me to it. They lifted me out of the van and onto a stretcher, and then they wheeled the stretcher away from the van, in case it caught fire.

Next thing I knew, I heard a whirling sound, and down out of the sky came a helicopter. They put me in the helicopter and flew me to Salem Hospital in Salem, Ohio.

When I got to the hospital, they medicated me for pain. A doctor looked over my broken legs. They were really messed up. The doctor told me that they didn't have the right facilities to care for me, so an hour later they flew me to Cleveland Medical Center. I was put in a room and given more medication. Somehow, I managed to fall asleep.

When I woke up there were doctors standing around my bed. They had the x-rays in their hands. They told me what they were going to do. The right lower leg was broken in the tibia, the bone in the lower part of the leg. They put a cast on that leg, and told me it would heal up okay. But the left leg was broken in the femur, the big upper bone that meets the hip. That one needed surgery.

They put a brace and traction on the left leg to stabilize it until they did the operation. By now the doctor knew that I had been through over eighty operations, so this was nothing new for me. He asked if I wanted to be knocked out with general anesthesia, or did I want a spinal.

"If you go with the spinal, you can watch the operation," he said.

I said I'd like to watch, I never saw an operation before, so he gave me the spinal, and I watched them as they set the leg. I remember the whole procedure. I watched him hammer in the pin with a rubber mallet, *bang, bang!* The pin held the broken pieces of the femur together. It was funny, I didn't feel a thing, the anesthesia was so good.

After the surgery they brought me back to my room and gave me more pain killers. I fell asleep. I stayed in the hospital from December third to the twelfth. My dad came to visit me. So did some of my friends.

On the twelfth I transferred to Providence hospital in Southfield for rehab. That was closer to my family, so it would be easier for them to visit me.

My dad visited me. So did my daughters and my brothers and sisters. Renee came every day. Everybody came to see me once I was in Providence. Yvonne called, and lots of friends, too.

My therapist, Gloria, said I would probably be there for a month, my surgery was very extensive. I still had the cast on the right leg. But I surprised them all, I was out of rehab in eight days. Gloria told the other patients what a hard worker I was. She never saw anybody work as hard as me and get out so fast.

I couldn't waste my days in a hospital or a rehab center. I had things to do.

A Sunday morning before going to Sunday School. Front row (left to right) - sisters Jackie and Gwen, brother Tony; Back row (left to right) - Brother Albert, myself, and Brother Luther

Left to right - Friend Toby, myself, brothers Tony and Luther. Picture taken 4 months before accident.

...with Dad

Myself with plastic surgeon Dr. Ian Jackson the day after surgery #108.

Gordy & Colleen - Mr. & Mrs. Hockey® & Rocky (the dog), Renee & me. (Photo by Del Reddy)

Above: Myself with Drew & Mike, two great guys of radio station WRIF.

Right: Les Brown, Del Reddy and me.

Tim Sheard and me.

CHAPTER THIRTY-FOUR

One day I was out in Troy selling candy at Whole Foods on Coolidge and Maple. A police officer came up to me and told me I wasn't supposed to be selling candy in front of the store.

I told him I had permission from the manager of the store. I wasn't bothering any body; I wasn't blocking the door or getting in the customer's way. I wasn't trying to push my candy on anybody, either. I just held the candy in my hand, and if somebody wanted to buy it they came up to me.

The officer said he didn't care if I had permission or not, I couldn't do it.

I said, "Well, okay," and I rolled my wheelchair toward the parking lot. I asked someone to help push me back to the van. A customer went up to the officer and told him off, saying "He's not bothering anybody, why can't you let him sell his candy?" But the officer didn't pay him any mind.

A friend of mine who was with me that day, Keith Thomas, had driven me to the mall. When he saw the officer speaking to me he came over to see what was going on. Keith helped me back to the van and we took off.

I talked about it with Renee. I was disappointed. And angry. The people there were friendly. It wasn't like anybody complained about me; nobody ever did that.

Renee said, "It seems like some people just want to make trouble for somebody else." She made us both a cup of coffee I was still drinking Sanka like my mom used to make. Renee asked me over her cup, "Are you fixing to go back to Troy?"

I told her, "Yeah I'm gong back. I'm not gonna let that policeman scare me when the manager is letting me work there."

About two weeks later I went back to Troy. This time Renee drove me. I went to a Farmer Jack store on Crooks and 14 Mile. The same officer pulled up. He got out of his car and came up to me. He was a middle-aged guy, pretty good sized man. I'm just a stick figure in a wheelchair; I'm not in a position to argue with anybody.

The officer said, "I told you you couldn't sell candy here."

I said I had permission from the manager here, too. "Why do you want to bother me? I'm not causing any trouble?"

"You're blocking the door," he said.

"I'm nowhere near the door. Nobody's complained about me, have they?"

The officer said, "I don't care if they complained or not, you're not selling candy in Troy."

"Well I sell candy in other towns. Police officers even buy it from me. There are even some officers in Troy that bought from me."

He said he didn't care who bought what. "You have to have a permit to sell in Troy. It's the law."

"Where do I go to get a permit?"

He said I had to go to the City-County Building in Troy. I said I was gonna look into it, and I left again. I didn't want to make a scene, I just wanted to sell my candy and meet people and talk to them.

At home I was frustrated and upset. Here was the same officer keeping me from my work. All this crime going around, and this officer had a thing for me. I wondered if he was prejudiced, or was he just ornery.

I talked to my dad. He told me I was in the right and I should stick to my guns. His wife Gertrude—we called her Gert—was also very supportive. She was always good to me. A couple of years before I started selling candy my dad remarried a really nice lady. Everyone in the family liked her a lot; she fit right in. Whenever I had to go into the hospital she was always very supportive and caring, just like my own mother would be. She was good to my dad, too. Especially after he had surgery and needed help with his recovery.

Renee said maybe I shouldn't go back there anymore. But I had a lot of friends in Troy. They liked talking to me and telling me their problems; they felt good seeing me there. I wasn't about to give up on them.

A couple of weeks later I went to another store in Troy. This time I was at Livernois and Long Lake Road at a CVS. I had permission from the manager there, too. I was just finishing up my sales when I saw that same police officer drive up with a partner and park in front of a Chinese restaurant. The restaurant was right by the van that Renee and Walter, her cousin, drove me in.

It didn't look like the officer saw me. I waved at Renee to drive around and pick me up. I didn't want any confrontation in front of the store. I didn't want him to make a scene and get people upset.

Renee and Walter picked me up. As she got ready to pull out the officer came up to the van and stopped her.

I said, "Officer, it seems like you have a thing for me. People don't say anything about my candy selling."

He said, "People don't like you, they don't want you around. You block the door, you get in the way."

"I never block the door."

He said, "You've got two choices: you can take the money back in the store and give it to charity, or you can go to jail."

I said, "Officer, I don't see any reason to give this to charity, I'm trying to make money to pay for my surgery. You act like I don't have a right to make a living."

Renee put herself into it too, not that she got mad. She was calm and very polite. She asked why couldn't he give me a break.

The officer's partner didn't look like he agreed. He told me, "Delbert, I was hoping you would give up the money, but I can see why you wouldn't." He was very nice; very compassionate. But he couldn't go against his partner. I understood that.

The first officer said, "I'm taking you to jail."

They put me in the back seat of his police car, put my wheelchair in the trunk of his car, and drove me to the Troy police station on Big Beaver Road. Renee and Walter went home. I told them, "Don't worry about me. When I get out in the morning I'll call you and you can come pick me up."

When we arrived at the station, the other officers in the lockup were shaking their heads and rolling their eyes. One officer said, "He arrested you up for *what?*" But the arresting officer was a lieutenant, he outranked the others, and there was nothing they could do about it.

At first I thought the lieutenant was bluffing. I didn't think he'd really lock me up. Even the officer with him looked surprised when he had to lock me in the cell. But the lieutenant wouldn't back down, and I had made my stand. I had to. I had been through over a hundred operations; I wasn't about to let an ornery police officer keep me from working.

He charged me with soliciting without a permit. I was put in a jail cell by myself; it wasn't like *Law and Order*.

Renee called the station. I told her I was all right. I needed her to bring a hundred dollar bond in the morning. The bank was closed, so she couldn't get the bond that evening. I went to sleep on the bunk feeling like I was in the right and everything would work out for the best.

They gave me dinner, a couple of hamburgers from McDonalds. They weren't too bad. I needed help getting to the bathroom. The officer on duty was very courteous; he didn't seem to mind. He said what did he have to do. I told him if he would unzip my zipper I'd take care of the rest, and things went fine.

In the morning Renee and Walter came to get me. They posted the bond, and I was out of there. I didn't even have to go before a judge.

Renee had a cell phone. I called Kate Lawson at the Detroit News and told her what happened. She told me to go straight home and to stay by the phone.

As we pulled up to my house we saw the Channel 50 TV news van was already there! A pretty young reporter with a big smile and a nice voice interviewed Renee and me. She even gave us tickets to a circus for Renee's kids.

We went over what happened, with the camera rolling. They wanted to get a video of me showing how I sold candy, so Renee drove me and they followed with the van with the dish on the top. We went to another store in Bloomfield; we stayed out of Troy.

Before we left the house to go to the mall I got a call from two attorneys, Robert Lippett and Roger Myers. They told us to go to a Farmer Jack at North Campbell and Twelve Mile. When we got there the news vans for Channel Four and Channel Seven were waiting for us.

The reporters talked to the manager at Farmer Jack. The manager told them I was no problem, I didn't bother people, I didn't get in the way. The customers never complained about me. He said I was always a gentleman. Always polite.

The manager even told the reporters that when I stayed away for two or three weeks, a lot of customers asked him, "Where's the Candyman? He inspires us."

The interview was on the air that evening. Rick Fisher on Channel 50 began his news with the bulletin, "The Candyman got busted selling M&M's."

The lawyers representing me held four press conferences. People were calling in saying how I was never a problem, how they liked to talk to me, that I helped them with their troubles and they always felt better for it.

I was interviewed by Drew and Mike on WRIF. All my family called in to the station. Nate and the others came over as soon as they heard it on the news.

My case went to trial six months later. I stayed out of Troy until the trial. In fact, I haven't been back there since. I think that's unfair, a lot of people liked me there. It doesn't seem right that I can't see them.

Rather than go through a trial I decided, along with my lawyer, that I would plead guilty to soliciting and the charges were dropped. No fine. No jail time. No community service.

I told the officer that I checked into getting a permit to solicit and found I couldn't get one, I had to be working in a nonprofit organization. The lieutenant who arrested me told me he knew about the regulation; that was why he told me to do it: because it was impossible.

EPILOGUE

My name is Timothy John Sheard. I was born in New York City and grew up in New Jersey, just across the Hudson River. There were woods and working farms behind our home when I was a kid, and my brother and sister and I had a great time roaming the woods all summer long.

After graduating from college in 1970, I got a job as a nurse's aide working on the orthopedic ward at St. Joseph Mercy Hospital, in Ann Arbor, Michigan. I was living with my brother, Tom, driving an old Saab station wagon, and wondering what I was going to do with the rest of my life.

One of the long-term patients at that time was Delbert McCoy. Miss Haab, the Head Nurse, usually assigned me to him, thinking he would prefer to have a man bathe him and help him get dressed. It made sense, and so Delbert and I spent a lot of time together.

His skin was always dry, because most of the oil-producing cells had been destroyed by the burns, and he itched all the time. I'd rub cocoa butter into his skin to relieve the dryness, but his skin still itched him.

Sitting forward in a chair, Delbert would say to me, "Hey Tim, scratch my back, will you? Scratch that skin right off!"

When it wasn't too busy I'd sit with him and help him smoke his cigarette. We'd talk. He showed me the picture of his pretty young wife and two baby daughters, the pride shining in his eyes.

When it was time for him to walk, he usually objected. He wasn't steady on his feet, and if he lost his balance and fell he would be unable to reach out with his hands to break his fall. But I kept a hand firmly on his arm and made sure he didn't fall. We would walk the length of the hall, which was a fair distance, and then go back to his chair.

When he was discharged, I lost track of Delbert, as usually happens when a hospital patient goes home. Sometimes, when we get close to a patient and his family, we stay in touch, but it doesn't happen very often. Relations between staff and patient are usually temporary affairs, like shipboard romances. Delbert went home to Detroit, and I never expected to see him again.

A year later I left Michigan to attend nursing school in St. Louis. After graduation I returned to Michigan and worked at Harper-

Grace Hospital in Detroit. I met and married a wonderful woman, Mary. We moved east, raised two fine sons, Matthew and Christopher, and eventually settled in Brooklyn, where we live today.

Some where in the late 1980's, as I approached my 40th birthday (I'm 54 now), I got the writing bug. It's a malicious infection, one that hasn't been adequately studied or reported in the medical literature. There's a clear need for more research and more effective treatments. Maybe even a vaccine.

But I was bitten. I began writing about the patients I had known. Delbert was one of the first to come to mind. He had such courage and optimism. I was always surprised by his expressions of hope. He believed that he was going to win a million-dollar settlement with the Detroit Police and the Marathon Oil Company, and that he would be able to buy a little farm upstate for him and his family.

I wrote a story about him, and then I thought, What if I was lucky enough to place it in a major Detroit news magazine? If he were alive, Delbert might read it, and I'd be able to get back in touch with him.

It was a message in a bottle. A romantic gesture. And as luck would have it, a wonderful editor for the Detroit Free Press Sunday Magazine, Wendy Keebler, accepted the story. She edited the manuscript, making it tighter and a much better read. The art department created a beautiful, haunting layout. On July 31, 1994, the article, titled ALBERT AND THE ANGELS, appeared in the magazine. I'd changed Delbert's name, not being in touch with him. Then I waited to see what would happen.

One Sunday I was home relaxing with Renee and the kids, just taking it easy. I wasn't going to the mall to sell candy that day, it being Sunday.

The phone rang. It was Napoleon Ross. He said, "Delray, did you see the Detroit Free Press today?"

I told him, "No, I didn't see it. What's it about?"

He said there was an article in the magazine section about a guy who was burned in a dance hall, and it sounded like me. The guy was named "Albert," not "Delbert," but other than that, it was my story, or at least, a part of it. The burn victim was even treated at St. Joseph Mercy Hospital in Ann Arbor.

Renee went right out and bought the paper. She came back,

spread the magazine out on the kitchen table, and we all read it together. It was me all right. We were all surprised. We didn't know what to make of it.

Renee said, "Why don't you call up the guy who wrote it?"

"How would I do that?" I said.

"We'll call the paper in the morning."

And so we did. Renee called the Free Press in the morning. She got in touch with the editor for the magazine, Wendy Keebler. Wendy was very happy to hear from us. In fact, by the time Renee told her a little bit about me and what happened to me after being discharged from St. Joseph, the editor said half the people at the magazine were crying, they were so moved to learn that I was alive and okay.

The editor took down my phone number, and she called the author at home in Brooklyn, NY. He took down my number and called me at home later that evening.

That's when I learned that the magazine writer had gone into nursing. That was no surprise, it was obvious to me back in 1971 that he really liked taking care of people. He worked as a nurse in different places ever since he graduated from nursing school.

He told me that he knew it was a long shot placing the story in a magazine, but the gamble paid off, because I was alive, I was in Detroit, and I was happy to hear from him.

We got to talking about the old days, about Miss Haab and Jack the Physical Therapist and Dr. Feller and Dr. Herbertson. Then we made plans to hook up. About six months later he flew out to Detroit and we had a reunion at my house.

We talked about what life was like back in 1971, and what we'd been doing all these years. It was a really nice visit.

Several years later, Kate Lawson, a writer at the Detroit News, wrote an article about me and my candy sales. It was a wonderful story, very sympathetic. After that, my friends started telling me, "Delbert, those articles about you are so good, why don't you write your life story?"

I was thinking that I'd been through an awful lot. Maybe if I told my story, other people who had suffered might be inspired by what I was able to accomplish. Here I was, badly disabled, still needing assistance with a lot of things, but I was helping myself a little with the candy sales, and I was helping Renee to raise a second family.

My daughters had graduated college and gone on to become

professionals; they were my pride and joy. I was just as proud of their children: Kim's son Aaron, he's ten. Monique's sons Braden is five, and Jalen is coming up on his first year. All healthy and growing and full of energy the way kids are. My heart fills with joy whenever they're around. And I still talked with Yvonne. I was glad we could keep in touch, we'd gone through so much together.

Sometimes my brothers and sisters and my dad would stop over to the house. Renee would cook up a pile of food: fried chicken and greens and corn bread. We would watch some TV, or sit in the kitchen and talk about old times.

June started to talk about the time he took the fuse out of the fuse box and hid it, and my dad gave him a good whupping.

"You might've burned down the house," my dad said.

"Yeah, but I didn't. Nothin' bad happened," he said.

We all laughed about the dumb stuff we did when we were kids. The trips down to Grandfather McCoy's farm in Silverdale...The parties at Shorty's basement, where we met Stevie Wonder.

"*Little* Stevie Wonder. He was Little Stevie Wonder back then," June said.

"You were all little," my dad told us.

We talked about gambling at Johnny's, and playing ball in the snow behind the old house. We remembered the great music from those days, and going to the Motown Christmas Review. We talked about mama's cooking, and Uncle Treetop's, too, the way he made a mess of the kitchen while serving a fantastic meal. We talked about our favorite dishes and their best recipes.

We didn't just talk about the good times, of course. We remembered Ball's death, and my mother's dying of cancer. We talked about Uncle Treetop's death on Christmas morning, and how the holidays were never the same. My sister Jackie just got out of the hospital again, suffering from emphysema. We knew it would take her from us one of these days. Each day she was with us was a miracle. Each day any one of us was alive and part of the family was part of God's blessing.

I looked at my dad, still tall and handsome, and my brothers and sisters. I looked at the pictures of my daughters, now grown with families of their own. I turned around and watched Renee cleaning up the food and putting the dirty dishes in the machine, and I was so grateful that God let me live to be part of all this.

It seems to me that maybe this was the reason I was spared.

Maybe this was God's plan for me. I was able to raise my daughters and see them through college. I helped my nephews grow up and get good jobs. Fred, who we call Boo, told me recently that he never would have gone to Michigan State if it hadn't been for me staying up late night after night working with him on his studies.

From the day that I was burned, the doctors gave me a one-in-a-thousand chance of surviving. It seems like my survival shows that, if your spirit is strong, and if you have the support of your family and friends, nothing can stop you. I guess that's the thing I learned most. Nothing can stop a man when he has that kind of support and faith, no matter how much pain he has to suffer, no matter how many operations he has to undergo, and no matter how long he has to wait for his recovery.

My family, my friends, my doctors and nurses and therapists, and most of all my faith gave me an inner strength that has sustained me all these years. It's just like Nate always told me, it's not the outside that counts, it's what's inside you. In your heart. There was always someone to help me in my troubles, just as we were always ready to take somebody in who needed a hand. The depth of that love has always sustained me. It was love and faith that allowed me to survive.